MYSTICAL HEALING

MYSTICAL HEALING

The Psychological and Spiritual Power
of the Ignatian Spiritual Exercises

JOHN HORN, S.J.

A Crossroad Book
The Crossroad Publishing Company
New York

1996

The Crossroad Publishing Company
370 Lexington Avenue, New York, NY 10017

Copyright © 1996 by the Maryland Province of the Society of Jesus.

Printed in the United States of America

Library of Congress Cataloging-in-Publication Data
Horn, John (John Philip)
  Mystical healing : the psychological and spiritual power of
the Ignatian Spiritual exercises / by John Horn.
      p.   cm.
  Includes bibliographical references.
  ISBN 0-8245-1582-X
  1. Ignatius, of Loyola, Saint, 1491-1556. Exercitia spiritualia.
2. Spiritual exercises. 3. Spiritual healing – Case studies.
4. Discernment of spirits.   I. Title.
BX2179.L8H67   1996
248.3–dc20   96-10347
                                                        CIP

...to Juan Diego's Mother and Ours,
Mary the Lady of Guadalupe,
Cause for Joy

CONTENTS

FOREWORD

Readers of this book will be doubly enriched: first, by the focus of the study and research on which it is based and, second, by the spirit and perspective of the author.

We live in a time when spirituality has surged into the consciousness of many Americans, moving far beyond the walls of Catholic or Protestant churches. The annual writings and hundreds of workshops devoted to spirituality range in quality from the profound to the shallow, and even the tawdry. We need authentic introductions to classic spiritual traditions written by people who know by study and by deep experience that of which they teach and write. In this book you will find a rich way of entering into the depths of the experiences of persons who have engaged in the Spiritual Exercises of St. Ignatius, in both the thirty-day residential and the 19th Annotation formats. You will be introduced to the dynamics of this strong tradition in Christian spirituality by one who knows the Exercises thoroughly and who understands the topography of the human soul intimately.

Fr. John Horn, S.J., D.Min., brings a strong academic and priestly formation to his study of the impact of the Exercises on persons' lives. Focusing his in-depth interviews with men and women whose experiences of the Exercises concluded more than a year before their talks with him, his case studies not only give us vivid windows into the movements of people's souls, but also provide a reliable assessment of the long-term impacts of their participation in contemplative prayer with Scripture and their being directed in the Ignatian retreat. I was moved both by reading the transcripts of Fr. Horn's interviews and by the insights he drew from his analyses of the ways participants' lives were affected. Honest and modest in his conclusions, Fr. Horn has given us a rare opportunity to look into the hearts of ordinary people who have been involved in extraordinary conversations with the Spirit and the Word of God.

JAMES W. FOWLER
Professor of Theology
and Human Development
Emory University

ACKNOWLEDGMENTS

A word of deep gratitude and thankfulness wells up within when I consider the myriad levels of loving relationships which both supported and contributed to this work. I especially want to acknowledge my Jesuit brothers in the Maryland Province. Their generosity provided me with valuable time and resources necessary for research.

Particular appreciation expressly goes to friends in the Lord whose care and humor radiates facets of divine love: Michael and Sue Abromaitis, Rev. George Aschenbrenner, S.J., David and Lura Barnes, Rev. James Borbely, S.J., Rev. Gerard Campbell, S.J., Sr. Rosemarie Carfagna, O.S.U., Mark Clarke, Sr. Maureen Conroy, R.S.M., Dr. Mary Lynn Dell, Msgr. John Esseff, Rev. Stephen Fields, S.J., Dr. Richard Fitzgibbons and the colleagues and staff of Comprehensive Counseling Inc., Rev. Richard Gabuzda, Rev. John Haughey, S.J., Jen and Ed Hogan, Bonnie Hurd of Taskmaster Enterprises, Kathy Kanavy, Rev. Joseph Kelly, Susan and Ed Mathews, Sr. Suzanne Neisser, R.S.M., Mary Grace and Dave Phillips and their children, Rev. Peter Ryan, S.J., Dr. Margarett Schlientz, and the generous interviewees who participated in this project.

A special word of thanks is expressed for Dr. James Fowler's and Dr. Don Saliers's encouraging guidance. As colleagues, they included me in a rare synergy of faith sharing, intellectual acumen, and Christian joy.

My parents, sister, brother-in-law, and their sons provide that irreplaceable quality of heartfelt acceptance and love which catechisms refer to as "actual enabling grace." This work, as all of life, flows out of streams of grace upon grace. May Jesus Christ, font of all grace, be praised!

INTRODUCTION

This book describes personal experiences of healing mystical prayer. Stories are told as women and men reflect back upon their experience of God's Trinitarian love after having participated in praying through the *Spiritual Exercises,* a spiritual classic authored by St. Ignatius Loyola.

The healing impact of encountering Jesus' Spirit during the experience of the *Spiritual Exercises* is illuminated. It is hoped that the reader will be deeply encouraged by seeing the practical effects of a regular discipline of biblically based prayer.

St. Ignatius Loyola's classic provides a framework, "Guidelines for the Discernment of Spirits," through which healing grace and growth in the Holy Spirit can be pastorally diagnosed. This work invites both general readers and pastoral leaders into personal reflection that can enhance their understanding of discernment and healing as spiritual gifts.

Pastoral leaders whose creative imaginations guide policy and who desire to learn more about the ministry of Ignatian spiritual direction, as well as the ordinary Christian, can benefit. The chapter dedicated to "learnings and implications" is especially related to informing the church's missions of evangelization and ongoing spiritual formation.

Through an instrument/worksheet, "The Inner Heart of My Faith," interior affective movements were evoked to create personal stories of healing grace (see Appendix II). This narrative method of reflection breaks new ground in revealing the phenomena of religious experience at work in the heart* of the believer who has participated in the Spiritual Exercises. Two contextual settings for giving and engaging in the Spiritual Exercises, the "at-home" model (a twenty-four week program) or the "retreat house" model (a thirty-day residential program) are in the background of each story. This

---

*Throughout this book I will be using the metaphor "heart" to refer to the deepest place of relation and truth in persons, the seat of spiritual insight and the grounding in faith.

work links contemporary faith experience in the ministry of Ignatian spiritual direction with the need for a more focused and informed spiritual formation at all levels of Christian ministerial service.

Pastoral diagnostic assessments are offered following each story of healing grace (according to the theological framework of Ignatius Loyola's "Guidelines for the Discernment of Spirits"). These spiritual assessments examine the person's appropriation of (or failure to appropriate) Christ's healing graces. The self-reported interior spiritual movements in a person's heart are examined and diagnosed theologically (making use of Appendix I) while relying upon professional wisdom from bibliographic readings in the partner professions of developmental psychology and educational anthropology. This exploration reveals the utter nearness of God's care in practical everyday living.

The experience of making the Spiritual Exercises, by entering into the prayer and spiritual direction of a retreat, can be life transforming. Some of my former retreatants have described the experience as "expanding the mind and heart" and "making God's love personal, every day."

During the retreat, participants experience in their hearts God's invitations to be loved, reconciled, and called to live in companionship with Jesus' living Spirit. This entails some type of sharing in Jesus' passion, death, and resurrection while making the Spiritual Exercises. The paschal mystery is tasted through the image of God, alive in the retreatant's heart, being placed in dialogue with the experience of the Holy Spirit's consoling activity in this mystery. It is a mystery to be lived out in day-to-day faith following the conclusion of the retreat.

The Spiritual Exercises are a type of map, a map for the human heart to follow in prayerful meditation and contemplation. To follow these exercises, and their engagement of the heart, brings one into intimate contact with the living Spirit of Jesus, Lord of all consolation. If the book called the Spiritual Exercises is bought and read, the experience is dry, like reading a telephone directory. To actually experience the Spiritual Exercises one must follow them with a spiritual director who provides guidelines for entrance into an interpersonal dynamic in the inner heart, a dynamic that is evident in the inner direction and powers of human desiring.

As a fifteenth-century Spanish soldier, Ignatius Loyola experienced, amid his own desires for fame and glory, Jesus' Spirit indwelling and at work in his heart. During a period of convalescence after being wounded in battle, Ignatius's deep desires were honestly and generously allowed to be engaged in prayer with the scriptural Word of God, and he experienced a personal connectedness that transformed the inner direction of his desires. Awe and wonder were engendered as well as the desire to experience more of Jesus' love in day-to-day companionship. Ignatius experienced, amid his desires, the surprise of being pursued by a God who actively loves him. Ignatius discovered in the dynamics of human desires the abiding miracle of the indwelling presence of the Holy Spirit who desires and yearns for us to have an ever deeper relationship with Jesus. From this experience of discovery Ignatius wrote his map for the human heart's interior journey into God's Heart, the *Spiritual Exercises*.

The contextual settings for making these Spiritual Exercises bank on Ignatius's insights into the adaptability of retreat formats that help the retreatants see and experience for themselves the love of God active in their own lives. The "at-home," or Annotation #19, format invites the retreatant to a commitment of one hour of prayer in solitude per day over a period of twenty-four weeks. Frequent communion with Christ's eucharistic presence is encouraged. During those twenty-four weeks the retreatants meet with their spiritual director once a week for an hour or more to describe the experience of interior affective movements (spirits) alive in their hearts. The "retreat house," or traditional, format invites retreatants to a commitment of four or five hours of prayer a day over a period of thirty days. In this traditional format retreatants meet with the spiritual director for one hour each day to verbalize the experience of their heart's inner affective movements. Daily communion with Christ's eucharistic presence in this "retreat house" format is expected. The "at-home" format is experienced amid the ordinary busyness of everyday life. The "retreat house" format is experienced amid an atmosphere of silence for the entire thirty days. Each format is equally effective in providing intimate encounters with Jesus' Spirit and in establishing interior disciplines for prayer which activate long-term healing graces.

The answer to the question "Who can participate in the Spiritual Exercises?" is relatively simple. Any Christian believer can participate who acknowledges the inner desire to experience more of the loving presence of God. Certainly, the Spiritual Exercises are not meant for everyone. The time and willingness to commit oneself to either of the contextual formats are necessary. The personal ability and willingness to reflect on affective inner movements are also essential. Ignatius taught that people cannot draw consolation from prayer unless the human capacities for reflection and conversation about heartfelt interior movements are noticeably present. And if consolation cannot be drawn naturally from prayer, a person is not able to enter into experiencing the Spiritual Exercises (e.g., someone who suffers from serious scruples or clinical depression requiring medication).

In this book the focus is upon the former retreatants' response (or lack of response) to their inner heart's conscious experience of the Holy Spirit communicating in and through prayer. Retreat participants recall this experience from their retreat and articulate it in the present day. This articulation occurs after about one year has passed since the retreat. Chapters 1 through 4 are these verbal portraits. In the interests of authenticity the interviews have been minimally edited. To help preserve the style of the oral presentation ellipsis points have been used to indicate pauses.

Anonymity was promised if this was a desire of the person retelling the experience of God's healing love. Names and places may have been changed to protect anonymity. In the introduction to each verbal portrait, however, care was taken to present equivalent information from a wide range and variety of background characteristics purposefully represented in this pastoral research (e.g., gender, age, race, income and educational levels, marital status). Prerequisites for participating in the co-creation of this book included a day-to-day discipline of prayer following the retreat experience and attentiveness to regularizing spiritual direction.

Experiencing healing mysticism while engaging in the Spiritual Exercises assumes a theological interpreting of biblical truth, namely, that human beings are born with innate capacities oriented toward conversation with God as Trinity. Each person, "whether or not the experience is noticed, carries within, a Trinitarian existential, rendering basic experiences of the Trinity."[1] The ability to communicate with and be touched by Jesus Christ, in the power of the Holy Spirit, belongs to each person. Knowing and appreciating these capacities in one's being produces interior freedom and increases joy in our hearts.

This work also assumes that true Ignatian prayer helps the retreat participant appropriate the biblically revealed healing friendship of Jesus Christ. The theoretical issues in this book are related to the former retreatant's being able to descriptively name highlights of personal inner-Trinitarian communication. In either contextual setting for the Spiritual Exercises, the experience of a deepening faith relationship with Jesus' Spirit, the kingdom of God among us, depends in theory upon the quality of a former retreatant having listened for, noticed, acknowledged, conversed with, and responded to inner affective spiritual movements in prayerful communication.

Readers are encouraged to pastorally assess and diagnose the narrative portraits to explain and find new meanings around the visible phenomena of spiritual growth. The accompanying charts are designed to assist in this exercise. They outline the commonly accepted healing dynamic of Ignatius's Spiritual Exercises which undergirds each of my enumerated learnings and implications described in chapter 5.

"Considering each story as a portrait of God's healing grace, it is especially pertinent to emphasize that each work of art has its own evidential force and power to convince."[2] You as reader will probably find one or two of the narratives in chapters 1 through 4 more appealing. These elicited appeals can further speak to your own heart. Through them I invite you to acknowledge your own interior affective movements calling for some attention in prayer.

> Because stories are verbal portraits they have the same power as pictures, sometimes more. Stories take us into other worlds, other times and places, just as pictures do. They point beyond themselves and invite us to follow.... When we stand before Van Gogh's "Peasant Shoes," we do not stand before it but in it — in fact, in them, in those shoes. You feel the earth, your tired bones, and the dying of the light.[3]

The verbal portraits in this gallery can simply be read one dimensionally as something that *we do*. But I encourage the reader to allow these beautiful and powerful portraits *to do* something *to* the heart as you permit them to carry you beyond yourself into receptive spiritual conversation with God. A series of questions at the conclusion of each chapter is listed to help readers enter into focusing on their own interior heartfelt appeals evoked by the narrative portraits.

In terms of contemplating the biblical Christ, the question needs to be asked, "Why is Jesus as Beauty so often unnoticed, so often not seen effecting change in human hearts?" After all, in Jesus Christ creative power itself resides. The answer is somehow a corrective in-

**The *objective* of "the enemy of our human nature"
is opposed to God's objective in each "stage" of a person's
development, growth, commitment in grace.**

THE ENEMY'S OBJECTIVE		THE LORD'S OBJECTIVE
enslavement through fixation	*The "first stage" – when a person is in a state of "bondage" (First Week Rules #314)*	conversion through conscience
turning back because of difficulty	*The "second stage" – when a person is striving to respond to the Lord (First Week Rules #315–27)*	growing stronger by staying on course
regressing through diversion	*The "third stage" – when a person is listening to and following the Lord in choosing between "good things" (Second Week Rules #328–44)*	growing union through simple progress
blocking through scruples	*The "fourth stage" – when a person has a sensitive conscience*	freedom in trusting the Spirit's inspiration

vitation. "If someone fails to recognize and appreciate the sculpture of Michelangelo or the music of Mozart, this is more a judgment about him or her than about the work of art. The same is true of the form of Christ, and Christ is his own measure."[4]

The corrective invitation for evangelism in the church is to invigorate its teaching of how believers might become more like little children, allowing innocence and humility to distinguish us (Mark

The Effects of God's Initiative Contrasted with "the Work of an Enemy"

In the "second stage" of a person's growth in grace, the effects of the "evil spirit" on the person's "state of soul" are obviously different from the effects of the Lord's Spirit.

The "enemy of our human nature" seeks to move a person more into a "state of desolation," in which it is more difficult to choose the Lord's way.	The Spirit of the Lord seeks to move a person more into a "state of consolation," in which it is easier to choose the Lord's way.
Temptations are more "violent" and seem to have greater force. By making progress more difficult, the tactic of "the enemy" is to turn a person back from the course of action chosen in a time of grace.	Inspirations are encouraging, supportive, empowering, harmonious. The tactic of the Lord is to lead the way one step at a time in the course of action chosen in grace, making the cost of adherence bearable.
When a person is attempting to make basic progress in the way of the Lord, characteristics of desolation include	When a person is attempting to make basic progress in the way of the Lord, characteristics of consolation include
troubled mind darkness not of God discontent agitation, disturbances apathy fear disruption sadness anxiety boredom inertia restlessness inner impatience with the Lord dejection (focus on self) self-pity involuted/convoluted reasoning dissipation of energies discouragement	peace of mind lightness of heart quiet/inner rest conviction conviction courage harmony joy zeal simplicity of action expansiveness holy desires patience hopefulness singleness of heart simplicity and clarity of thought focused energies self-acceptance
diminished vitality of faith, hope, love increased susceptibility to temptations	increased faith, hope, love increased ease of spiritual progress

10:15). Affective imaginative prayer takes us into the preconceptual
world of being like children. Yearning for such knowing to multiply
within us found Blake concluding:

> If the doors of perception were cleansed, everything would ap-
> pear as it is — Infinite. But the doors of perception are hung
> with cobwebs of thought; prejudice, cowardice, sloth. Eternity
> is within us, inviting our contemplation perpetually, but we are
> too frightened, lazy, and suspicious to respond: too arrogant to
> still our thought, and let divine sensation have its way.[5]

Praying according to the dynamic theological method of the Spiritual Exercises promises practical mystical experiences, a knowing in
faith that reverences each person's subjective make-up. This interpersonal method, however, presupposes Jesus' saving grace as Love, as
Beauty, irreversibly grounding and affecting humankind prior to and
beyond our subjective inner life.

> All of the asceticism that accompanies prayer thus receives its
> focus. Its aim is not to make persons and things disappear from
> view; rather it purifies the relationship of the heart to all that
> exists, so that the heart may be where its treasure — the Lord —
> is. The decisive question for prayer is not the local or mental
> space it inhabits, but the presence that dwells in that space. This
> presence is in the heart as on an altar on which the Holy Spirit
> places and engraves the eternal Gospel: Jesus.[6]

The more prayerfully attentive we are in heartfelt conversation
with the biblical Jesus, the deeper is the exchange and healing trans-
formation. Our quality of living increases. And when believers' lives
are more radiant and appealing, we walk in the everyday as living
portraits announcing Christ's reign. May our hearts abide in and
radiate the living presence of Jesus.

Chapter One

ARLENA'S EXPERIENCE OF HEALING PRAYER

Profile

Arlena, an African American, age forty-one, lives in North Phila-delphia and works as a medical assistant in a poor neighborhood where high unemployment and drug-related crimes are common. She continued her education after high school by pursuing business and medical skills training, as well as obtaining college credits in religious education. Arlena has completed two years of college. Currently sep-arated from her husband, she proudly raises a daughter and a son as a single parent. Their involvement in an inner-city Catholic gram-mar school engendered a desire to join the Catholic Church because of feeling part of an extended family in faith. Following Arlena's experience of the Spiritual Exercises in the "at-home" format, she continues to pray about an hour a day, partially in the morning, partially in the evening. The experience of relating to God in the Spiritual Exercises continues to deepen within Arlena's heart through "realizing the true me,... realizing that I am being transformed daily through the Holy Spirit to be the *real self* that God created."

Interview with Arlena

John: "Arlena is an active member of the Gesu Parish. She has provided me with a background sheet of basic information about herself. And I'm very grateful for this time to have a conversational interview. So, Arlena, the first question is, 'What was the greatest or one of the greatest experiences of God's love during the Spiritual Exercises, as best as you can remember?'"

Arlena: "Oh, as best I can remember. I think it was basically the love of myself. I am a person that ran around doing for other people all of the time. I love to give, but I didn't like to receive. And during the Exercises . . . it's like sometimes I felt very dark inside like God was not present there. And I wondered why. It made me cry. It brought up a lot of feelings of anxiety, you know, anxiousness. I'm saying . . . that I know God is here with me and God is present, . . . but what's the greatest thing that I'm getting from this. Well, it was knowing that I did not love myself. I found that out . . . that I was guilty . . . I would spend time on anybody or anything else. . . . I wouldn't spend time on me or for me. . . . If it had to do with me, self, I just like . . . you know . . . I was a thing. I didn't exist because God created me and loved me, . . . that's how I felt. I just existed to do things for other people. To be a caretaker sort of, . . . and that really hurt. I actually cried during those times of the realization that, you know, all this time I didn't love me. I didn't put anything into me and yet I wanted to become closer to God. I had to first love me and then I knew that the relationship with God could become deeper. I felt that way afterward. . . . And it's truly felt because I had to know that I loved me and cared about me and some of those things that I was doing for other people, . . . like giving to them, . . . I had to now be able to receive. And I was. I opened myself up and I think it was a lot of pride that was there . . . and it was put there as a child growing up, you know. Where you do for people and you do this and you don't worry about yourself, . . . God will take care of you sort of thing. And that's how I grew up. God's going to take care of me. But how is He going to take care of me if I don't take care of me? If I don't love me first of all. And I think that was the greatest thing, . . . one of the greatest experiences."

John: "Can you say anything about how you responded to that experience of God's love?"

Arlena: "Well, I started to just look at me and say, you know, God loves me . . . and I love me. Now that I realized, . . . you know, . . . God created all of us and the thing that I did for me . . . was just got deeper in prayer and became closer to God. I asked God to show me the graces that I needed to know. . . . You give me the wisdom and the knowledge and the understanding. You teach me to pray, to pray better. It's like almost that I could pray by myself sometimes, and I knew what I wanted to say, but to other people at times I just couldn't say it. I didn't want to get up there and say that. But one of the greatest experiences was when I became president of the PTA. Father George came in and said, 'Oh, there's nothing to it.' You can do it. And I said, 'Well, I guess so.' And he would do the prayer for the first two times and then the next time I said, 'Well, Father George, aren't you going to do the prayer?' He said, 'No, you do it.' And I ... Oh, God, ... so I started, you know, ... it was the first time I did the Our Father. And that was okay. No problems. He said nothing. The second time I would bring my little prayers in and I would read them. About the third time, I started thinking, God, ... I asked you to help me. Just help me to pray. And I got up and I actually prayed. And I prayed from my heart. I prayed from what came from within me to all of the people. They might have felt that it took me forever to say that prayer. But afterward, some of the people came up and said, 'You know, you pray very well. You do a very good job. I thought, thank you. You know, ... not knowing that I could do this. And that was one of the things that I wanted to do was to be able to pray out loud and around other people. And that was one of the greatest things. And it helped me to know that God's love was there and that's something that I really wanted. ... And God has granted me many graces since then."

John: "So here you were doing something for others, but for yourself first."

Arlena: "Yes."

John: "You were in that leadership position and yet you tapped into the grace of what God had shown you on the retreat."

Arlena: "That's right. That's right."

John: "Now were you PTA president after the retreat or during ... ?"

Arlena: "During. During that time I was PTA president. But I would always bring my prayers and read them, you know. And that was acceptable. That was okay. People liked it and Father George never said anything. But I just ... I wanted to do it from my heart. I wanted to do it from my feelings, from the experiences in my life. And I was afraid. I was afraid. And ah ... the only way to get over fear is to put fear behind me and know that God is right here present with me. And if I ask for help, God's going to give it to me. And I ask, 'God help me to pray.' And I got up there and I did it. And I really ... I was afraid. I was still afraid to do it, but the fear was so strong that, ...you gotta do this in order to get over this because you want to do it. You know, it was something I wanted so much to do...and then I was able to do it...and I felt good afterward. And I was a little scared,...you know. And then I just kept doing it. You know, the more that I could get up openly and pray from my heart...pray for what I was feeling, from what's happening in the environment in the country, in the world. Those were the prayers that I brought before the people."

John: "Can you say,...It's so rich,...what you're saying. Can you say a little bit more about when you cried,...about loving yourself? Can you say more about what that was like,...about what you experienced?"

Arlena: "It was pain....It was like devastation....It was like knowing maybe you lost a loved one and you're thinking that loved one is never going to come back again. It was that kind of pain. The realization that God truly loves you and I didn't love myself. How could that be? How could I exist and not love me? Well, that's what I was doing. I was just existing. I didn't have the love in my life that I wanted or needed. I wasn't shown that. By God, I was shown that love. During the Spiritual Exercises the things that came up...the sinfulness,...the guilt,...why didn't I love me. I think I felt some of those things in my life, and I was afraid....Well, God doesn't love me, so how can I love me? And when I realized that God loves me above all things, through the sinfulness, He forgives me....And He's still there. It's not that God turned away from me at all. God was with me all the time. I didn't recognize His presence."

John: "So the tears were,...the crying was the devastation being,... Was it being taken away?"

Arlena: "Being taken away from me. My life at that point there. There was no love for me. And I just cried, because I said,...'God I do love me, I do love me....' And I never showed me love. It was that I had to do for everybody else,...to say, well, this is who Arlena is....She's this person that does all of these things for all these people and that made me up. But...deep inside there was a yearning for something different,...for something closer. To be closer to God,...to be more intimate with me,...to know that God was all things to me. He was brother, sister, lover, you know?...And that was hard in the beginning to even envision, to imagine,...that God was all these things to me. But God was the comforter that I needed in any area of my life. If I needed that brother or that sister or that lover, you know,...that friend. You know, that person just to be there with me in that quiet time,...that peacefulness,...God was there."

John: "And is that sense of God's presence still with you?"

Arlena: "Yes. Very much so. It's put Him in my everyday life,...because I spend time now in prayer with God each day. I have to start my day off like that. I get up extra early just so I can have that time. I spend that time in the evening, too, because I like to reflect over my day. But knowing that through everything,...that God works,... and He's working in my life,...and He's walking with me through this journey every day no matter what happens. I accept with joy whatever happens in my life,...because it's a change for me. I can see that God is transforming me in every area of my life. I think differently,...that I used to be judgmental or I didn't want to speak up about certain things. I have to do that for me now. You know, these things were just...brought out the things that really made me up with the true self and that's the person that I was hiding from the world. Nobody knew that person but God. And I think it tells I didn't want God to know that person. I was pushing Him out of my suffering and out of my pain. And that's where I realized I needed Him most and need Him there. And I didn't want Him there,...because I thought that He should be in the good times and the happy times. And during the Spiritual Exercises I learned that God should be in that pain and suffering. How you gonna get above it? But God's right there with you, you know. You need something...a foundation ...and God is that foundation of love."

John: "You mentioned this pushing away of God during times of pain and suffering. Just to continue on with what you are saying,... Can you say more about what you came to understand,...what you understand now about what we might call resistance to God's love, or sin, or however you want to interpret it. How did you,...do you, ...push away God's love?"

Arlena: "Well, if I think that I've done something very sinful,...you know, it's like I'm ashamed...I'm guilty. But I want to keep this intimate relationship with God. So, I have to go to God and ask for forgiveness. I push God away at times when I think Arlena can do it, the self, the ego, can do this all by herself and I don't need God. And God has shown me in many ways that lots of times in my life, . . . that if I come to Him and I pray and I ask for something and it's good for me, . . . God gives it to me. An example is, I prayed very hard about getting certain people out of my house at one time, . . . when my son was locked up in jail in a different country, . . . and God gave me the answer to that prayer, . . . by telling me to contact this certain police-man. I didn't want to do that. I said to God, 'You help me and I will follow whatever you say.' As soon as I got up from prayer, the self stepped back in . . . oh, . . . that's okay you don't need to go get this policeman. And I said, ah, . . . but I just asked God to help me, . . . so I've got mixed feelings of resistance that I do want God there, but I don't, . . . you know. And I got on the bus, going to work, as usual, . . . got off at the wrong stop and who comes out of the deli but the police officer! And I was shocked! And all I could say was, 'Thank you, God, and I will never, never ask you to help me again and not listen to you.' And I asked this policeman for advice and he said, 'Sure I can help you. I can do it right now.' And he was there, he was available, . . . everything that I had asked in prayer that morn-ing, . . . happened that afternoon. And that was like, a miracle, . . . you know. And God has had many miracles like that in my life, for me, . . . that I prayed for an answer for something and the answer was being right there, and these were times when I didn't want to accept what God had said to do. But I had to keep coming back to God, . . . asking God to help me and my dealings weekly, . . . to understand and to have the humility, . . . for Him to give me the grace to listen to Him and to obey. I think I didn't like to obey."

John: "Let me ask you how you know when God's asking you to do something? You're obviously very attuned to things going on inside now.

Arlena: "Yes."

John: "How do you know when it's God asking you to do something in that true self?"

Arlena: "Well, what I do in my prayer is always ask God. . . . I say, God there is nothing that you and I can do today that cannot be handled. Whatever we do in this day, you are there present and we can do it together. And by that I mean, . . . I take myself and I push myself aside in the prayer, and I let God's Spirit work through me. I feel it!"

John: "And what does that feel like?"

Arlena: "That's, oh!..."

John: "Take your time,..."

Arlena: "I don't even know how heaven feels, but if I was an angel and I had wings,...and I could fly to heaven or wherever the presence of God might be in my life,...I think I would be very light, very joyful. I have a heart of love, pure energy and understanding, ...because God has given me that grace to quiet myself to be able to listen to what's being said to my heart. He speaks to my heart. And when I try to do it logically, I mess up,...every time. And by that I mean,...things just don't go right. They don't go the way they should, if I ask God, 'God you help me and I'm going to sit here and I'm going to listen to what you say to my heart. Speak to my heart. So I talk to God,...and then I quiet myself and I listen and I feel what's happening to me,...the feelings,...the emotions....If it's a feeling that I don't understand or that I might not like, I ask God to explain that to me. Why am I resisting at this point? Is it a lesson that I need to know? Something I need to understand? It's just that God helps me understand it,...because my presence is there with Him and I feel like we are one. We are connected, you know, in my prayer time. I feel that there is nobody or nothing else there. Nobody but me and God."

John: "The pride that you mentioned,...you were mentioning that you were praying to listen and be obedient....Can you say anything more about how you push away,...or what's in the pride, you know, ...without analyzing, but just describing it?"

Arlena: "Well, I think that the pride that I'm talking about is selfish sometimes. I may want certain things for me and they may not be the best things. I might accumulate a lot of material things and I feel that, 'Well,...God, I worked hard for this and you gave it to me.' But, for example,...I put a lot of pride into my car. I worked very hard. I got the money and I bought the car,...and three years I had the car and then I ran into financial problems. Certain money had stopped financially, my hours were cut back and I didn't have enough money to keep the car. And the pride was,...well, I'm going to feel so ashamed and embarrassed in front of people when they say what happened to your car? You know?...So I said, well,...how am I going to feel when this man called me up on the phone and said you need to pay your car note and I can't pay it, because I don't have the money. I sat and I prayed to God and I said, 'I'm hurting inside and there's pain inside and I know that it's this earthly pride that I have,...that this is mine and you gave it to me,...and you helped me get it,...and now you're taking it away from me.' But I put so much energy into my car. Fixing it up, putting these things on it,...these expensive alarm systems on it so people wouldn't steal it again,...because I've had this happen to me. And yet, I saw that I spent so much time on the material things in my life, and it's as though I didn't give God equal time to those material things. They were more important to me, you know,...because I accumulated all of this. And the first thing that happens is that my hours were cut back, I lost money, my car was repossessed, and I said, 'How am I going to explain this to all the people who ask me what happened?' I said, 'Well, the bank took the car back.' And the first time I said it I thought well,...I wonder what they are thinking. Wow! She didn't have the money to pay for this, and she just came right out and said it. There was nothing else for me to say because I had prayed to God about it. And I said, 'I don't know what to do except tell the truth and the truth, is I couldn't afford it. And the truth is,...that I put so much time and energy into having these things that I wanted,...and not much time into my prayer, because my car would take me here and do this for me, and I didn't have enough time for God. I didn't spend the time...You know? Oh, I thanked God for giving me these things, but it was like, 'Oh, you gave me this. This is mine now.' And myself just took over,...and it's like God just quieted me down and I went on retreat....I remember at that time, and what came to me was,...Sister Suzanne had asked me, 'What are you asking God for at this time in your life?' And I thought all night long and I says, 'I can't tell her anything tomorrow because He ain't told me anything but humility...and I don't even know what that means.' Well,...when I sat there and I told her this, she said, 'Oh, do you know what that means, Arlena?' I said, 'no.' I said, 'but nothing else can come to me,' I said. 'I've been praying all night long. I didn't even sleep good because I'm trying to think what do I want to tell you tomorrow. But when I finally let go and relaxed,...God spoke to me,...and the only thing was the humility, honesty, and truth.'...

You know? And that's basically what I wanted in my life. I was tired of covering up for everything in my life. You know, I always tried to make things right for my family members. I'd fix it. I was a fixer. You know, I'd fix everything for everybody so everybody would look good. I didn't want my husband to look bad because he did these abusive things to me, or I wouldn't argue in front of the kids with him. But yet I had all of this anger, ... all this anger. You know, and this was pride, because I wanted to look good in front of everybody. And I no longer want to do that. I want to be seen just as I am, ... the way that I am. And I hope they discover the true me because that's who I'm discovering, the true self."

John: "And what's this feeling like, of being connected to God when you're listening and being obedient? I would like you to have a little pause and think about how you experience what that's like now, ... that relationship, ... you know, in the day to day, now. Maybe you could just describe that?"

Arlena: "Okay, but ... "

John: "I mean, I know you have already, ... and if we've gone to the limit, fine. But can you say any more about what that's like now?"

Arlena: "The connectedness with God is that when I get up every morning and I have my prayer time with God, ... it's like I don't even want to end it. It doesn't feel I'm here on earth. It feels like I'm lifted up so high in this prayer and in the time that I spend with God, that we are so connected. ... We're connected in love. We're connected in an intimate relationship and it's so important for me to have the love of God and the peace and understanding, and the joy that I want in my life, ... and yet I see every day that I'm struggling. But in that struggle God is there present with me. It's not a struggle that I'm being alone in, ... in the activities of my daily existence. God is there with me. We're connected because I won't let go of God. You know, I want that presence of God in my life and in everything that I do. I'm willing to stand up for me and I think that most of my life I wasn't willing to do that. I would just let things pass over and think that they would be okay. ... You know, they would die down. But now it's like I've gotta find me in all of this and the only way to do this is to stay close with God, so that God can continue to speak to my heart. And God's in other people. It's not all the time that God will give me an answer right there in prayer. There might be a person who walk up and say something to me that day,...and a light bulb like goes on,...that's what I prayed about! And this person is saying this to me! How did they know that? And I'm saying well,...an angel of God is always present, because we are all children of God and we can all bring a message to each other. So that connectedness with God is very strong in my life, each day, because there's always somebody or some-thing I could speak to,...be obedient to in nature and all around me and everything and it's because I'm no longer judgmental also. I would judge people and I would say,...that's not right to judge people. But I don't do that any longer. I...immediately,...if it comes in that I'm judging somebody,...I ask God to help me to see the people as He sees them; to love them as He loves them."

John: "Arlena, in the Scriptures there are these stories of Jesus,... whoever He seems to be with, He heals or touches people. How would you say,...and it's all right to say,...if you didn't experience healing,...but putting that in your own terms,...How would you say that you experienced Jesus as healer? You mentioned a comforter earlier. And specifically,...how do you regard yourself now in that connectedness with,...with God? So, it's really two questions."

Arlena: "Okay,...well, God as healer, one example for it, this month and last month I've been having very, very severe headaches. And I figure,...well, maybe it's just stress, maybe it's just tension because of all of the things that I'm going through in my personal life right now. I wanted to make sure that nothing was seriously wrong with my head up here, you know? So I took sinus medicine, I took pain medicine for tension headaches and this would die down,...and by the end of the day I was in severe pain again. So it was very difficult in praying when you are in pain, you know. But because I can pray and I can put that pain aside and let God come into it and just heal me,...I feel that we are all great healers to ourselves because through the Holy Spirit, God gives us that certain power to be aware of our own bodies, to be in touch with our bodies. I started doing acupressure and only through prayer did I remember even to do it. It is something that I learned to do years ago. I wanted to get rid of this sinus headache and so I touched certain points in the forehead, you know, the hands, the legs to get rid of this tension and the migraine, ...even in the top of the head. And I'm saying, 'Boy, this pain went away.' And I think, you know,...if I had listened earlier I could have got rid of some of it, but I did it unconsciously. I would sit down and I would massage the pressure points in my head, . . . not realizing that I was doing it. And it's because I had already asked God to take this pain away. To show me what was causing it, you know? So I'd go and I'd go through this expensive MRI test on last Thursday. The test comes back fine. There's nothing wrong with me. You know what I'm saying? Well, every time there's some physical problem with me, it's been very hard for the doctors to find it. I really think that I did a lot of praying that they could find out what was wrong with me. And a lot of times it would end up as my decision. So I would really have to pray to God, 'Should I let them cut me and go in there and look and see?' You know, I've had that incident of the gall bladder, . . . and took very sophisticated tests, and it showed nothing. And the surgeon said, 'Well, Arlena, I don't know what to tell you. You'll have to think about this.' He'd say, 'I think it's your gall bladder. You've got all of the symptoms and you've been suffering for eight years, almost ten, and now you're in severe pain and you really can't eat these certain foods. But we can't find anything wrong with you.' Well, I said, I gotta go pray about this. And I did. I went home and I prayed. The next day I called him back and I said, 'You can operate.' And I could do that because I knew something was wrong and I knew they couldn't find it and I was aware that God was going to heal me and get me out of there. When they went in, . . . the whole gall bladder was stuffed with infection. They took the whole gall bladder out. I didn't have gall stones like people usually have. . . . The whole gall bladder was diseased. But because I can listen to God speak to me and saying, 'You're going to be all right,' you know, . . . 'if you have this surgery' . . . I went on that. The same way with my back operation. When I first went they said, 'Oh, you need bed rest for a month.' I took that off work, . . . I come back and I can't stand on my feet. I'm in terrible pain. They're telling me, 'Oh, it's just a lumbar strain or low back strain.' Well, then I got the MRI and it showed I had a bulging disk, but it was still up to me to get surgery or think that maybe physical therapy would do it. I said, 'No, I want the surgery.' People would say, 'Well, you might be paralyzed. You're not going to walk.' I said, 'God's going to take care of me.' I was up and walking around that hospital when my doctor came to visit me and he said, 'What are you doing out of bed?' I said, 'I'm fine.' They couldn't believe how miraculous my body healed because God was healing to me! I was not afraid at those times. And I think the times that I've had fear in, . . . I didn't let anybody touch me. You know, I

had to pray to God, and it was something simple that if I changed
my diet or did something, I would be fine. God has been healer in
many ways to my emotions. He's healed a lot of pain and anguish
from childhood abuse from my life, you know. He's healed the physical pain from my body, and I trust,... I won't do anything unless
God speaks to my heart and tells me, you know. And when I did the
acupressure and been relieving some of the pressure, the headaches
haven't been as bad this week. And I wondered, Why couldn't I have
done that before? I think God wanted me to see that if you asked
me for help, I'll help you. I did all the physical things on earth that
I possibly could, you know the medical things, to go get the MRI
done, take the medication and I got no better. When I listened to
God and started doing something for me, just applying simple pressure, I got rid of the headache pain. Now it comes and it goes, but
it's not severe like it was."

John: " ... doing something for you?"

Arlena: "Doing something for me, ... what God helped me to realize,
... that I could do this for me through God's power. I didn't do it.
Arlena didn't do it. I did it because I was guided to do it. So I feel that
God and I, we do things together, and that's how we stay connected.
You know, we work together, ... on everything, in all issues of my
life. I know God is right there, you know."

John: "Does anything... does anything, standing back, ... standing
back a little bit, ... does anything else stand out or is anything else
highlighted when you think back to making the Spiritual Exercises?
You've said so much that's really rich."

Arlena: "Yes, there is ... "

John: "What I mean, Arlena, ... is as an experience of God's love."

Arlena: "Yes. I remember when we were doing the Spiritual Exercises, we were asked to be a person at Jesus' death, you know, ...
to participate in that death. And how we felt as a person that participated there. Who were you and how did you feel, how did you
react? Well, what really got to me, is that the pain and the suffering
that Jesus felt on that cross, ... it was like all the pain and suffering
in my life just hit me. And I didn't know what to do. I was crying when I came downstairs, ... because I would usually go up to
chapel, you know, ... we had different spaces in the house to go to

and have our quiet time. And I chose the chapel and I sat right there near the altar and tears started coming and I'm saying, 'This feeling, I don't like this feeling.' I really didn't want to talk about it when I came back downstairs when the group got back together because I really felt bad. I felt all this pain and suffering that Jesus did is like the pain and suffering in my life,...but understand that Jesus died on that cross for all of us, for all the pain from all of us,...for all the sufferings that we might ever imagine. And I'm saying how can Jesus imagine what I'm going through, you know,...this is two thousand years later? And he rightly...I was very, very upset and hurt because He had died on that cross for me. I don't think I could do that, you know. In my humanness I'm sure I couldn't. But knowing that God...you know, Jesus was both human and divine,...of course He could. He did suffer so great for us,...that we take for granted. I think we only realize that during the Easter time season when we go through the death, the passion, you know the resurrection of our Lord. That's the only way that we really let Him touch our heart. But, you see, that touched me at that time and I think since then He's been touching me through all of the suffering because it no longer makes me ask the question, 'Why am I suffering so hard?' I just ask Jesus to come in there and be present with me because you already suffered for this. It's like all of these battles in my life, you fought them for me when you died on that cross and all of the victory and the happiness is mine now on this earth. That's how I feel. And that was just so outstanding,...I think that really stayed with me because it was just difficult for me to envision my Lord dying for all of these many, many things. But he really did!"

John: "And the tears again,...could you describe...you know tears can...there can be a lot of different things in tears. In your experience, in Arlena's experience..."

Arlena: "The tears were like pain and they were like joy. They were pain because Jesus suffered,...and because I suffer in this life. I would not like to suffer. They were joy because through this pain and suffering, He's healing my body. He's washing away my sins. He's in this pain and suffering with me today. He's not way up there somewhere,...He's right here walking this journey with me. He's on this path of my everyday life. And that's how I see Him and those tears were both pain and joy. And they were a wonderful experience, ...because when I cried, it was the pain and the suffering for Him, but also the pain and suffering for me. And it was like a healing took place inside of me,... because I could recognize the love and the peace in all of God's people,... you know, not just me. Because I no longer was the selfish person that I used to be. And the joy came because it's there for me every single day. All I have to do is accept it. I think acceptance was a big thing for me,... to accept, you know, from other people and even to accept these gifts from God. But I asked... I asked for them. I asked for the graces."

John: "Can you say,... I'm going to push you to the limit,... Can you say even more (and if you're at your limit, fine),... about what that pain and joy is like? Could you describe it a little bit more... what the pain and joy is like,... was like and is like?"

Arlena: "Well, it was bittersweet. You know, if you eat a sweet tart, how it is? You know... sweet and then you get to that center. It's like a bittersweet relationship. You know that you have the pain and the suffering. And I knew that the pain and suffering was there in my life. And I think that maybe I was angry because of it. I needed to let go. I needed to forgive people. I needed to ask God to forgive me for things in my life that I felt shame or guilt about,... for even people that I felt had abused me, you know? And during the Exercises, I learned that I could have Jesus sitting right there with me and I'm sitting here,... and I can bring that person in... that I want to forgive,... and I can ask Jesus to help me. Sometimes I couldn't even envision that person being there. I would just envision feeling the love of a newborn baby,... how a mother would feel so joyous and happy in the greatest gift of life... that one could be given. Jesus would help me do that because the presence of Jesus was there. And it was so astounding because the grace and the joy that I felt,... because Jesus could help wash away all of these things, and Jesus could help me to forgive that person. And I kept doing that with a child,... until I could bring a person that I truly wanted to forgive. And usually when I did this, it was somebody that was deceased,... that was in my life that physically or mentally abused me. And I, you know, ... I thought that I had forgiven,... and I really realized how much I hated, you know. And it was amazing how... after years these things would come back up in your life and you want to forgive. You know you want to forgive, but you as a human person can't do it alone. And you need some help, so I had to bring Jesus into that picture,... with me. First, it was like I would sit there and I would just talk to

Jesus about my hurt and my pain,... and the tears would come, and they were tears of suffering, because I hadn't forgotten, you know. I hadn't brought it to the surface,... and I think once I did that Jesus could come in and heal my heart. But I wanted to bring the other person's presence there to say I forgive you. And that was the pain and the suffering,... but the joy was that I could say,... and really mean, 'I forgive you.' The joy came in because it was like a release of something that you held on to... and Arlena didn't let go of it. She just held tightly and figured well, 'If I say that I forgive you because you didn't know what you were doing,' you know,... but really deep down inside I didn't forgive, you know. And Jesus can help do that ... could help me forgive."

John: "And the joy? What's it feel like now?"

Arlena: "Oh, the joy is... Oh... it... it... I'm so elated with the joy, you know! Joy's in my life every single day. And it truly is because I want it there. I want the acceptance of it. So when I can accept the joy, in there, then I get the peace and the serenity that I need. When I see things in my life today that might make me a little angry,... I can see that there's another side to it. There's the side of peace and love and the joy. The joy that... what it does... is it brings so much out of one's self. It's like I give myself totally to you, God, to do as you please. I ask that your will be done in my life. And that's my daily prayer,... and that brings me joy to be able to say, 'Well, God, you gave me this life and I can give this life back to you,... to use me.' That's a joyous occasion for me. And it's like,... it's there every single day,... because I constantly ask God, 'You use me, you speak through me, you know what's in my heart, you help me to articulate well,... to say what it is when these feelings come up, you know. Let me feel them,... let me be happy about it. And I am."

John: "Is there an image of connectedness between you and God that means a lot to you,... that portrays what God is like toward you?... And if there's not, that's fine. Some people have images; some people don't. But is there one that... "

Arlena: "that I have?"

John: "One that would be Arlena and God,... that describes this whole experience?"

Arlena: "Yes,...a true friend,...a true friend as I've never experienced on this earth. One that walks with me, talks with me, listens to me, but guides me. That image is just so strong with me because I can go to a friend and say, 'Well, this is going on in my life,'... and they'll give me advice. And sometimes I think friends just need to listen...because you just come in for support and you say, 'I need someone to listen to me.' Sister Suzanne sort of reminds me of that because she sits there so patiently and she listens to me. She's walked a great journey with me in my life. And she listens and she says, 'Well, Arlena, what would you say about this particular thing,... about how God is guiding you in this situation?' So she makes me think. She doesn't give me the answers,...she never has....She tells me to think about it. She tells me to pray about it. If something in particular strikes her in the Bible she gets the Scripture out and we'll read,...and I'll take it home and that's what I'll do those two weeks, ...with that marked,...depending on how often I meet her. But the image of God as being that true friend is that God is not judgmental. He's not going to judge me if I feel I did something wrong. And a friend would,...Could I actually come to a friend and say, 'Well, you know I did this?' I'll be thinking all of the time,...well, that friend is going to judge me and maybe I'm a little afraid and I won't say this part. I don't feel that this is a true friendship because I can't share it all,...I share quite a lot with Sister Suzanne, and I feel very comfortable in doing that, you know. And it started out just by having a conversation,...just like talking, you know, getting to know each other. And the last few years have really been fantastic because it's like I can go up and say anything,...and she accepts me as I am. And that's how God accepts me,...as I am and right where I am."

John: "Arlena, I'm just going to ask you to rely on that reflection worksheet that you did, called 'The Inner Heart of My Faith.'... Not to give back exactly what you wrote there, but just what you remember when I ask you some simple questions. And the questions are about your experience before and after the Spiritual Exercises. So I'm going to ask you to try to keep your responses brief here. And I'm just going to ask...(like for instance) the question about your philosophy of life. Could you say what your philosophy of life was like before the Spiritual Exercises and what it's like after; what it's like now?"

Arlena: "Well, before was just commitment to a lot of things. You know, other than God. And now it's like a commitment because I choose it to be close with God in all things every day of my life for as long as I live."

John: "And how about your greatest fears,...What were your greatest fears before the Spiritual Exercises?"

Arlena: "Well, it was almost like I'm never going to know who God really is, and God is never going to accept me as I am. I felt that I didn't know God as I wanted to know God. And I wanted to get to know God a little bit better and I think every day of my life is like,...I want more. I want more. I'm thirsting for knowledge and understanding of God's Word."

John: "Now think about this for a second. Now that you know God so intimately as a friend, and there's been such healing, there must still be some fears. What is your greatest fear now,...even though there's this incredible love affair between you and God?"

Arlena: "The greatest fear, I think right now for me, would be,... that if I came to God and I said something to Him and would feel very guilty about it,...it would mean to me that I have not really accepted God's forgiveness,...of whatever it might have been in my life. Or, the greatest fear is,...I'm afraid to go to God to tell God something, you know,...I want to be able to be open and not be able to hide as I once did before in my life. I mean, I wanted God to know this part, but I didn't want God to know that part....But God is all-seeing and all-knowing, so God knew it all already. It's that I had to be able to understand that I could come to God with any-thing. And my greatest fear is,...if I felt too ashamed or too guilty to come to God."

John: "How about your deepest experience of joy or gratitude before the Spiritual Exercises?"

Arlena: "Yeah, well,...my greatest joy and gratitude was always thanksgiving and praise to God, you know. I knew that God existed and I would thank Him and praise Him for the things that He did in my life. But I took those things for granted. You know,...and now I don't take them for granted. It's the praise and the thanksgiving that I can give to God from my deepest being when I can totally give God, myself,...just as I am."

John: "As experience in general, is there any one experience of your deepest joy and gratitude from the Spiritual Exercises?"

Arlena: "Yeah. Well, I think, for me I could put it this way. If I can risk something, and by that I mean,...I trust God and I ask for His guidance and understanding. If I can come up and say to you, 'Well, you know,...I really love you and I really care about you and I care about your feelings and I'm not out to hurt you.'... You know, if that person is out to hurt me and I'm not (and that's the situation right now in my marriage that is being dissolved you know,...because my husband wants a divorce)...it's that I don't hate him. There's no hate. There's no resentment there. Every day I pray for him. I send him God's love and peace and understanding, you know,...that God's going to get him through this. Because at the end of our marriage it's like...maybe he's beginning to realize this and to see all of the things that I tried to explain to him before that were going on, that he refused to see...And now that there's no closeness there that...you know, the communication part was broken and we separated from that,...it's that greatest experience that I can say,...'Well, I can still love you, but it's a different kind of love; ...one with peace and joy and understanding...and knowing that God loves you, too.'"

John: "This might tie in with some things you just said. I'll just ask it. Your deepest experience of sorrow before the Spiritual Exercises?"

Arlena: "Well, my deepest experience was,...I felt a lot of shame and guilt before the Spiritual Exercises,...and that was in my childhood family abuses situation. I really got,...I felt unclean before God,...that God would not accept me. Yet, all of these things that would happen to me were not my fault. I couldn't understand that. After the Exercises, after doing them,...you know, being involved, ...I said, 'God loves me and accepts me as who I am. God forgives me,...and He shows the light and the love of even that person that did this abuse.'...You know, and that was the hardest thing for me to try to get within my being....That I really had to work on with some therapy sessions for about a year. I did that,...constant praying and my spiritual direction. I had them all going at the same time to help me through this because I didn't know how deeply that I was hurt...how deeply I had been wounded. But during the Exercises it helped me to realize that God is present in all things. And God never left me. It's at that time I think I pushed God aside, ... because I didn't want Him there in all of that, ... because I thought I was unfit, unclean, unhealthy and I didn't want God in that part of my life. I only wanted Him in the happy times, ... and there weren't many happy times. So, it's like as I got older, because I was raised going to church, singing, worshiping God. . . . I knew that God existed and I knew that was the only person that I could talk to about my life. God was always there for me to talk to. But I always knew that God was at a distance then. I didn't understand that God was not at a distance. He was always right there with me. But I wasn't taught that so I didn't know that and I didn't understand that."

John: "What would you say was your deepest desire before and after?"

Arlena: "Well, my deepest desire before was I wanted to get to know God. I wanted to get to know God, ... and I just wanted to give me to God to use as God saw fit. And usually, ... like I thought maybe helping God's people that didn't understand God's Word, ... to bring that Word to those people, ... to help them to understand, ... and I do that every Sunday morning right here in this room with the children. . . . You know, and I never thought that I would stand here and teach children God's Word. But this is how I feel that God is using me. That's what God is doing for me in my life right now. And before there was just that desire that God would use me. And now God is using me! I'm saying, 'All right, God, come on, use me some more.' You know, I still want to do ... this thirst for knowledge, it's always wanting to get closer to God, closer to God, closer and closer. You know, the closer you get and the more knowledge and understanding you get, you want a little bit more. You say I don't have enough."

John: "And the last question in this before-and-after way of looking at things is ... (in some ways you've answered it), ... but can you say what was your way of regarding yourself before the retreat and after the retreat?"

Arlena: "Sure. That's an easy one and the reason why it's so easy is because before the retreat I had no self. I had no true self. I was everything for everybody all the time, ... and it's like I wanted something more and I didn't know what it was. And I had to come to grips with, ... I had to love me to love God because God created me and He created me out of that love. And during the retreat and after the retreat it's a realization that...I did come to grips to love me, ...and I did understand that self-worth was important to me. And the self-worth,...was that I didn't have it before. I didn't care about me. I didn't matter. Other people, other things mattered. Now, it is that those people and those things...they still matter in my life,... but I also matter because I worked on finding me through the Spiritual Exercises,...through spirituality, through going to school for the religious education courses that I'm taking,...I spent two years and some for the church ministry program,...just to get to know more about God. And I still go just to get to know more about God's Word. I feel it and I want the people to feel it when it's coming out of my mouth. So those are the graces and things that God has given me ...and I feel good about me now,...because I'm doing things now ...that I want to do. I'm making choices for me,...whereas before, if somebody said, 'Can you do this,'...Yeah, I can do this,...You know, and maybe I didn't want to do it, but I did it because they wanted me to. Now, I do it because I want to. And I say no, and I don't feel bad about it anymore. I used to have this real guilty feeling if I said no to you,...you know, you would not like that. And I would just do it to put up with you. That was like limiting myself to something. And I no longer do that. I go for just what I want. And I won't settle. I was settling for anything before and by going through the Spiritual Exercises,...getting to know God better, getting to know me,...that I'm a very special person. I'm special,... because I now love me and God has always loved me."

John: "Arlena,...that's beautiful...it's a beautiful summary statement. If someone walked up to you on the street or someone from this parish was considering making the Spiritual Exercises, and they said to you on the side, 'Arlena, what's that experience like?' What would you say?"

Arlena: "Well, I would say the experiences that I had when I took the Spiritual Exercises was enlightenment of God's Word, God's knowledge...that God could take Ignatius, a soldier from years and years ago and change his heart, the conversion part...just like God changes our hearts as He transforms us each day. To go through this, ...to know that all those years ago God loved and gave people insight...He changed their hearts...He changes our hearts now so that we can become more loving, caring and understanding. I think that it would be worthwhile for your spiritual growth in understanding... because that's how one truly grows,... is by getting to know God's Word,... getting to feel it inside and practicing it every day of your life."

Summary

Arlena's desire to grow closer to God was felt, acknowledged, and is being generously attended to in her day-to-day life. Engaging in prayer according to St. Ignatius Loyola's Spiritual Exercises provided a watershed experience in faith. As Arlena allowed herself to quiet down inside and to be honest about her inner feelings, she encountered a felt absence of God accompanied by deep anxiety. Remaining faithful to prayer in the face of this experience of desolation bore great fruit. Amid the battle between her true self and her false self, Arlena discovered that she can open herself to experiencing healing peace and joy by not "pushing God out of pain and suffering." By meditating, especially on Jesus' passion, the Holy Spirit teaches Arlena's heart about God's love and friendship always present caring for her. This heartfelt lesson evokes tears through which great sadness dissipates. This lesson also engenders a growing confidence and strength to stand up for herself, to be free from materialistic concerns, to be able to engage in public speaking and to forgive people who had previously abused her.

Jesus is experienced as "brother, sister, lover and comforter." Instead of relying solely on ego strength, coming to Jesus only in the good times and with positive feelings, Arlena allows herself to stop managing her pain and to relate sufferings with God in prayer. In that interpersonal dynamic a sense of "being washed" is experienced as angers, hatreds, shame, and guilt are released. Arlena experiences improved physical health, grounded in a growing self-love. She ends up in a dynamic self-offering to Jesus in friendship. By allowing her imagination to bring Jesus' love into painful memories Arlena continues to taste healing grace as she feels Jesus "suffering with and for her." A whole new self-regard and ability to exercise self-love is a gift that Arlena enjoys now more than ever before. As a result she even finds herself able to love enemies, her abusive husband, and others. Overall, her experience of Jesus' unconditional loving heals and places her heart in a nonjudgmental posture within human relationships.

Especially worthwhile to note in honoring Arlena's revelatory experiences of desolation is the Guideline for the Discernment of Spirits #314. Here Ignatius Loyola explains that a "sting of conscience" will be felt deep within the retreatant when a fundamentally lovesick dimension of the person's heart is addressed by the Holy Spirit's impulses as indwelling Word. For Arlena, a root desolation becomes evident and the sting of conscience occurs when she is asked to meditate upon Sister Suzanne's question, "What are you asking God for at this time in your life?" She experiences a sleepless, restless night during which a call to discover a personal meaning for "humility" is evoked. Frustration surfaces. Core anxieties face Arlena from within a heart that did not know how to receive basic consoling love around painful memories of innocent suffering.

After a night of wrestling with her inner conflicts, one of the tactics of Satan, the enemy of human nature, comes to light. Previous impulses that will carry Arlena to "cover up" sufferings and angers are seen as impulses which, when followed, bind up and prevent Arlena from receiving deepening discoveries of her true self. In Guideline #326, Ignatius warns that Satan often inwardly suggests covering up interior realities that are embarrassing, much like a false lover who promises false security and pleasure if secretiveness is maintained. Arlena responds generously to the Holy Spirit's upsetting sting by choosing to honestly face and bring to light her fear that Jesus would not be present in the middle of her core pains and suffering. Arlena tastes enormously consoling love as she exercises real humility. Pains and sufferings begin to be touched by the healing light of Christ's presence, her true lover and friend. Humility begins to be defined incarnately in Arlena's felt understanding.

Two vital points of creative tension can be seen in Arlena's narrative portrait. First, future relating to herself-in-Jesus calls for an interior vigilance, allowing deepening healing grace to be appropriated, by watching for and fighting against attitudinal and behavioral patterns which take Arlena into not admitting inner pains. These tendencies can promote unrelatedness with Jesus as "brother-sister-lover-comforter and friend."

As Arlena's spiritual growth unfolds, crafty tactics from the evil spirit can be anticipated, most especially around the old wounds and scars from having suffered emotional and physical abuse. Any extra well-intentioned busyness, amid the church's needs for leadership and Arlena's emerging gifts, must be subject to ongoing discernment.

Extra activity can easily feed the false self's patterns of avoiding and covering up hurts.

Pleasures and consolations derived from giving up material goods can be subtly imitated by the evil spirit, too. These heartfelt movements need to be scrutinized since there may be unhealed dimensions of Arlena's relating to herself as a victim of abuse and as an African-American woman living in a culture besieged by racism. In other words, any further simplification of lifestyle in Arlena's newfound freedom from material concerns needs to stem from authentic heartfelt impulses that continue to bring about increasing love of self and personal freedom through Christocentric self-denial. Inviting Arlena, in regular spiritual direction, to name the accompanying heartfelt movements attached to her experiences of consolation and desolation will provide necessary spiritual guidance and caring companionship as well as a taste of Jesus' desiring to complete her joy (John 15:11).

General Questions for Personal Reflection

1. How does Jesus' Spirit speak in your heart? Name and articulate a few recent experiences in faith.

2. Describe the heartfelt inner struggle between your true self and your false self in relating with Jesus.

Specific Practicum Questions for Spiritual Directors

1. In your own words, specifically describe what you see and understand to be the healing dynamic of Jesus' Spirit at work in Arlena's heart. Name the points of her strongest felt consolation and desolation.

2. As you read Arlena's story, what were you experiencing inside yourself? What happens when you take these inner affective movements to Jesus in friendship?

Chapter Two

EMMETT'S EXPERIENCE OF HEALING PRAYER

Profile

Emmett, an Episcopalian priest, lives and serves in a multicultural, lower-middle-class parish on the outskirts of Washington, D.C. He comes from a poor white Southern background, is fifty-four years old, and is very happily remarried after suffering the death of his first wife. Emmett is the proud father of two young children. He holds a Master of Divinity degree and has participated in some postgraduate doctoral studies. Following the "at-home" format for entering into the Spiritual Exercises, Emmett felt and responded to Jesus' Spirit's personal call to take a public vow of nonviolence. He prays on the average about an hour a day and describes the overall experience of the Spiritual Exercises "like waking up after a bad dream...like returning home after a difficult and dangerous journey...a coming home."

Interview with Emmett

John: "Let's just let this be as natural as possible....So, the first question is,...Emmett,...could you describe...as best you can... the greatest experience of God's love during the Exercises...or one of the greatest experiences of God's love? Could you describe what that experience was like?"

Emmett: "Probably the greatest experience of God's love during the Exercises for me...and it was a surprise...because I had started out with some specific things in mind...and then other things opened up...was a growing self-acceptance,...that I looked at...things in my life where I judged that I had failed or been inadequate...and

32

found that God did not need to beat up on me about that,...and indeed never had. And that also, I didn't have to either. So He was going to help me not do that. The form of the experience, I think, had to do with...Gerry Campbell's gentle...and unforced progress ...toward moving from one day to the next,...and seeing where the Exercises were leading and where God was leading me,...leading me into trusting...that God would lead me somewhere even when I didn't know...where."

John: "Could you describe any specific experience of that self-acceptance that...you know...how it came through in your prayer ...or in your practical experience during the retreat...how that came home to you?"

Emmett: "To answer this I have to go back a little bit and talk, about some of the things that were going on in my parish...some of the conflicts that were going on in my parish around...around issues of race...and misconduct issues...at an earlier period...in the parish's life,...where I became sort of the focus of the anger...of a group of people...who had been very much the leaders of the parish,...and had to...kind of accept that...and live through it,... that there was no way to argue with it, no way....I had to come up against people who could look me in the face and say...'I just don't like you,'...and to try...to try...to accept that,...not buy into it, but to...accept that and go further...and continue to be a faithful pastor to those folks,...but also continue to move...steadily...toward the development of the multicultural reality of the parish that I serve,...development of the leadership of people of color...and minorities in the parish...and allowing them to claim their space, ...and to...*knowing* that that ministry was the right thing to do. So, my...the experience of the love of God there was...a kind of walking on eggs...and trying to do all these things in relation to all sorts of different people,...not having...not being willing to...to sort of create sides...and have a group that was for me,...because there was already a group that was against me,...but to stay out of that...and to not...not create a group behind me,...But to allow the dynamic to work itself out, and to work itself out in me...and on me. It was...a willingness to...and I feel it was a gift of God... the willingness to allow all of this conflict to be played out...in me ...and around me...without my...buying into it. Does that make sense? Is that helpful?"

John: "It makes sense, but I'm going to ask you if you could say a little bit more about just that...the dynamic working on you and in you,...the experience of God walking on eggshells....Maybe if you could say a little bit more about that metaphor,...it'll just naturally come out."

Emmett: "The great temptation is to say, 'I'm right,'...and there- fore,...I will gather people and persuade them that I'm right and we will walk over...the people who think something else. And...to say,...I can neither walk over the people who think something else, ...nor gather followers...because I'm not here to gather followers. This is not the *role* of the priest in the community. We're supposed to all be followers of the same person,...and to stay with that,... to stay with the biblical base,...to stay with the sacramental cele- brations,...to stay with the pastoral care,...while the temptation is to be defensive,...to be self-justifying,...to say, 'Look God is on my side'...And I think it was God's gift to me...and with counsel and help from Gerry,...as this is going on,...looking at why I'm here,...what my vocation is,...whether I have a vocation to a more specific vow of nonviolence....All of these things were getting af- fected around that...and to walk with that...and to *feel* God, not making it all right for me,...but being with me in my experience of it being what it was,...which was both a test and a desert and an endurance."

John: "And God being with you...through the desert, through the endurance, through the self-acceptance that comes...that being with you...was like... ?"

Emmett: "The being with me was like a...there's a phrase here that I will quote, 'I've always lived in this desert.' I was a very solitary child...and solitude is a pretty natural state for me...And so...to know that it was all right to be in solitude,...to live in a culture that is hostile to solitude,...but to know that that was all right. One of the things...one of the dissatisfactions that people felt with me was...that I was not...enough of a glad-hander,...not enough of a hail fellow well met. They would say, 'You're not warm enough, you're cold.' And my experience of myself is *not* that of a person who's cold, but I do enjoy my own company and...I don't have an easy time making small talk with people. I can talk about things that are serious for them, ... whatever they are. But, I think, I'm straying from what you are looking for."

John: "The question was, ... God being with you or you being with God ... as the dynamic was working on you and in you ... with Gerry encouraging gently and (of course I'll push you to the limit). So, ... if you've said everything you can say, that's fine. You did answer it. You said that there was this ... deepening of self-acceptance of the goodness of solitude in a hostile world. But can you say ... anything further ... even in reflecting back, you know, ... for yourself now, ... of what that *being with* was like or is like?"

Emmett: "There was one wonderful moment with Gerry, when he got to a part of the Exercises ... about examining a choice that had been previously made ... or making the choice all over again. And I said ... I really need to remake the choice ... the decision to come to Ascension Parish again ... because I think that was probably a disordered choice. And he just sort of sat back very gently and said to me, ... 'What makes you think it was any more disordered than any of your other choices?' And while the question in its content could be devastating ... because it's the clear implication that all of my choices are disordered, ... and they are! ... The way it was formed ... enabled me to say, ... the fact that I make disordered choices ... means that I'm a human being. And I seek to make more and more ordered choices, ... but there's not a point ... at which you get to where you just automatically make ordered choices ... and after which ... you never make any more disordered choices. So, that was a really *root* kind of thing about self-acceptance, ... the fact that my self-awareness is ... in many ways ... deluded, ... The fact that I con myself and kid myself ... about all kinds of things, ... seemed not as devastating ... as it had seemed before. So ... that I didn't have to deny ... that I was doing it ... in some cases. And therefore, ... and I think in practical terms, ... not having to deny that I delude myself ... sometimes, ... makes it ... possible for me to be little bit less self-deluding. And that I experienced as *enormously accepting* ... on God's part, ... that God accepts me even though I'm a character who's capable of deluding himself ... and gets me to the point where I can see that ... and in that very process ... helps me to begin to be a little bit less self-deluding."

John: "And how does that register in your heart... in the feelings of your heart?"

Emmett: "Well, it makes me feel,... good. And... it gives me a sense of solidarity with other people. There's a wonderful image... that Martin Smith quotes... from a film of the baptism of Jesus, by John, ... and all of the religious iconography has John standing there and Jesus standing there... isolated... John's baptizing Jesus,... And in *this* film... Jesus is swimming in the river with hundreds of other people... and the baptism is... He goes into the water *with* other people... and enters into... our fallenness... and takes on our need to wash ourselves... and be cleansed. And that sense... that solidarity with other people,... that's part of what that sense of acceptance means,... that I don't... that I am not some kind of character who is... better than somebody else,... better than the rest of God's children,... and so not in need of forgiveness,... But *neither* am I... a character who *has* to be better... than somebody else. Neither am I somebody who *has* to be purer... and nobler... than anybody else. I can... God can use... me as I am,... no better and no worse than other people,... but with *particular* gifts... that are... some of them are pretty interesting."

John: "From your heartfelt vision of it,... how did this affect... the way you wanted to be in the parish... amid the conflicts... and being one among the people in that sense of following Christ with them? What happened in you... and in the parish community that was part of this experience of the retreat?"

Emmett: "I think it's a double thing. One,... that I was able... to stick to my guns... as it were... to say this is the course I'm going to follow... because I think it's right.... And to do that,... while being told by some people, 'don't do that'... and by other people, ... 'Oh, my goodness,... if you do that these people are going to be mad,'... And the sense of... well, when I came to the parish it was about 30 percent nonwhite... and there was a *rhetoric* of acceptance of diversity. But the overwhelming leadership was white... and suburban and middle-aged people, who had moved out to the suburbs. And this area.... which was a suburban area thirty years ago,... is now a 50/50 mix... black and white area,... And one of the realities of church life in the Washington diocese and in this area of Washington, D.C.,... is that there are historic black churches...

that people can go to, who want that,...And there are, of course,
...plenty of overwhelmingly white churches that people can go to, if
they want that. And there are a handful...especially out in this little, little area,...just north of the District,...of parishes which are
seriously multicultural. So that both the white people and the black
people...who come here...have to want to be...in a place that is
mixed....And so...I sort of took that,...I took it at its face value
and assumed that everybody had bought into that,...that they were
as attracted by that as I was,...that I didn't want to raise my children in an all-white community. And most people had,...but the
group that had run the parish...for many years...that had gotten
rid of the rector before last...and brought in the guy that had left
before I came,...really wanted to stay in control...And were not
open to that....And *now* the leadership is 50/50, black and white.
There's an African member of the vestry...there are a couple of
West Indian members of the vestry...there are African Americans
...as well as assorted white folks, liberal and conservative and all
...all kind of others. So that I was able to say,...Okay, this is the
right course of action...and I'm going to stay with it...no matter,
...you know,...the fact that people disagree with it is okay. They
can disagree with it. But the other thing was to...to be able to accept,...to know that I did not have to be perfect in doing this,...
that I'm a flawed human being...entrusted by God with the ministry...in this place. And that...it's not a matter of...once I get
to be absolutely pure and perfect, then I can do some ministry. The
ministry gets done...by me and by others...as we're in the *process*
of being purified,...which is longer than a life-long kind of process.
And my experience of God *in that*...was of...well, of coming to
accept God as a loving Father...of becoming *at ease* with the Father image,...which I'd not been at ease with...for a lot of reasons,
before,...and letting God be that for me. Not necessarily...insist-
ing that that image be the one for anybody else in the world, but
nonetheless...that was the way in which God was reaching me and
caring for me...and...accepting me...and bringing me. I think I
told you...at one point...I was praying over in the church,...and
we have a choir and there's a little stall where I sit to pray,...and
just sitting and looking down at my feet where the kneeling bench is
...and *seeing* my son Nathaniel,...at age three,...just lying there,
and, and, and,...experiencing God saying to me,...'I love you...
the way you love him,'...Because I hadn't had the experience of

loving a child...that way before...so I couldn't have known that
...until that happened."

John: "Do you want to say anything further about that experience
of the Father's love and...what it was like then,...whether it continues now....It's sort of like boring into a gold mine in a way, you
know?"

Emmett: "Well, what it was like then,...it certainly continues now.
Let's see if I get any help from this sheet."

John: "So the question was,...if you wanted to say anything further
about the experience of God's love when you...(or what you heard
in your heart)...as you saw your son there in front of you?"

Emmett: "Well,...I cried a good deal...at that particular moment.
It was not embarrassing. One of the things that I've learned...is
that people do cry in church....And I make it my business to try
to help them...not feel embarrassed. There's something about...the
connectedness with God,...even though...even people like you and
me...who are professionals at it,...don't have it all down...and
are sometimes ashamed of it. There's something *there* that opens us
...to God...and therefore, there's some crying to be done. So, I feel
okay about that. I have a lot of experience of tears of joy. I don't
cry so much when I'm sad...as when I'm just overwhelmed with the
love of God....And it just runs. It just pours. So *that* sense of...
knowing myself to be God's son...and a brother of Jesus...is part
of it. How it continues is...in a kind of dailyness,...a kind of quo-
tidian quality. There's a wonderful hymn of John Keeble's,...'New
Every Morning.' You know,...that God...that God will...that the
trivial round, the common task...will give us all we need...to offer in sacrifice,...to accept His blessing...to experience God's love
and God's grace. And so *finding* myself *content* with the ordinary
...was one of those major graces,...of finding that God is here...
in this very ordinary little parish...for me...that I don't necessarily
have to go someplace else and be a big muckie muck...or a member of the hierarchy...in order to serve God greatly...as Ignatius
talks about,...that the *greatness* of the service...is in the quality of
the service, not in the importance of the job. And so...that sense of
acceptance...was part of it...and continues to be...a part of the
experience of God in the Exercises."

John: "Shifting gears a little bit,... could you describe an experience ...or whatever the greatest experience was of inner resistance...to letting yourself receive God's love.... Try to describe that experience from the retreat...or in the present?"

Emmett: "Well, the resistance,...I think the greatest resistance to God's love...in my life has been,...has been my strength. I grew up as a poor white kid,...in the deep South. My father left home when I was about five. My mother had my younger sister and me to take of...and worked as a school teacher,...and her parents living in the same house.... So we grew up in a three-generation household, which was a blessing...in a way,...but there was not a lot of attention to go around...when I was a small kid. And so *survival* was the mode of operating...that I developed. It seemed like it was difficult for me to survive...and so no matter what happened,...I survived. And that ability to survive, to survive poverty...to survive a terribly racist society...to survive the lack of resources...to survive expectations that were...pretty low of what life was like...to survive a kind of early and constant sexual hunger for women...and frustration in that. So *survival* became the mode...and when my first wife, Carol, got sick and died,...I think I went back into that survival mode...a lot...and in a way...had to...to survive. And yet,... that survival mode is not an open one. It's not one that is open to God's grace,...not one that is open to seeing God's hand at work in ...in the terrible things that happened to us,...or the pains and the losses of life. So...part of the gift to me...was the gift to be able to *feel* lost,...without being lost...myself...and to not have to survive,...to trust that my survival was not my responsibility,...that I didn't have to do that...that God was going to do that for me. This is new. It's just coming up."

John: "It's very beautiful. And so...the experience of resistance is... is a tendency to stay in that survival mode, I suppose? How does God ...generally or specifically...how do you experience God breaking through that...or inviting you out of that?"

Emmett: "I had a lot of experience of God *laughing* at me,...of suddenly seeing the absurdity...of what I'm doing interiorly,...that here I am...not only taking care of myself,...but taking care of the world, taking care of my family, taking care of my congregation, taking care of the universe to make sure that it doesn't collapse in on us. And...then suddenly...it just seems *hilarious*...and here's this one little character...that's supposed to be doing all of this stuff... and isn't doing it. I'm not doing that. And God...is not stepping on me like an ant,...but is looking at me...and smiling and laughing at me...sometimes crying with me,...and saying,...'Come on boy,...you don't have to do that...I love you...and you have stuff that's worthwhile.' Partly,...and I think that this is kind of typical of men of my generation,...men in their fifties...American white men in their fifties,...that I'm responsible for...everything,...especially that women feel all right. And if a woman feels bad...then it's my job to make her feel good. And to learn that I *can't*...do that,...but what I can do is to be with somebody in the pain that they've had...and relate to that...because I've got some pain... that I've had. That was a great learning. I think...when we were driving back from Louisiana...this last trip a couple weeks ago,... stuff always opens up from childhood when I go back there,...as you might imagine. And, as we were driving along,...everybody (the two kids and Anne) was asleep in the car...and I was just driving along...and I thought about my late wife...and how sad that was. And I thought,...I'm never going to stop feeling this...you know. I've been married to Anne for ten years. Carol's been dead for twelve. I'm never going to stop feeling that loss...that pain. But it doesn't devastate me. It doesn't destroy me. It's possible to feel it...and not have to hide from it...and that's God's love...and acceptance... except that I couldn't keep her alive. I remember once thinking,...if I could, I would die for her...and yet God doesn't give that to us... most of the time. You know, you might die trying to save somebody from drowning,...but somebody is sick and dying of cancer and you are...the beloved person who is there...and you say I wish I could die for you,...but you can't. You can kill yourself, but you can't... save her life. And to know that that's always going to be there,... but it's not...it's not debilitating...it's not destructive. It becomes a vehicle...a place that God can use to...to anoint me...and to just pour oil."

John: "Anointing is a very evocative word. What heartfelt knowing goes with that? How do you feel as you experience God anointing you...in that nondebilitating experience of pain?"

Emmett: "The language that I have for it is...is fairly abstract. It's the language of acceptance...and stuff like that,...but of being loved, of being held, of being...cared for,...of being nursed. There's a wonderful Greek icon of Panagia Galactotrophusa...the all-holy One,...the giver of milk. And it shows the Virgin Mary with her breast exposed expressing milk...down in an arc...into the mouth of the infant, Jesus. I think that in some ways and in some parts of me that's who I am,...a person that needs to be nourished that way. In other ways and in other parts, I'm a fairly strong, supple person, capable of...taking care of others. But what I think the Exercises...were the occasion for...was getting some clarity about the ways in which it is appropriate and possible for me...genuinely ...to take care...of other people...without having to protect them from life,...without having to intervene as a kind of...brittle armor...to keep the pain of life from inflicting,...from visiting other people. That I don't have to protect all of these female characters in the world...from life,...that I can help people with some of the realities of life,...but not protect them from the pain of life."

John: "I want to ask you, Emmett,...to go back...just for a bit to the God laughing with and at you image....And you've already described what that experience was like. Can you say anything further about...what God laughing at you is like?"

Emmett: "It's a very *intimate* kind of experience. It's a...for one thing,...somebody who is laughing at you is in relationship with you. And the laughter...the laughter...is not like God makes fun of me. There's nothing...none of that. But like an engagement... an acceptance of here I am...pretentious, foolish,...trying to keep running things that don't need me to run them. And He comes in and sort of says, 'It's okay, you don't have to do that....You can relax and you can experience my love....You can let Me love you.' There's something in one of the letters of John,...'Not that we first loved God, but that God loved us first.' And maybe it's the Protestant side of my upbringing that...that...love of God and love of neighbor is an *obligation.* It's something that *I've* got to do. But, *in fact,* John says that we only can love either God or each other *because* God has loved us first. And the experience of God laughing ...gently and warmly...at me...is an experience of knowing that I can stop trying to generate out of my guts all of this love...because God is, in fact, loving me...and out of that love...comes all of the love that I can or need to...produce in response."

John: "When we talked prior to this interview, there was a song and an image (that has come back to me as we're talking now). It's something like...the hands that uphold, or...underneath are the everlasting arms. I just remembered that that seemed very important as a...descriptive image of what the experience of God's love in the Exercises was like. Could you describe that a little bit,...why that image...why that experience is appropriate...and what the experience in general was like?"

Emmett: "There are two things,...the Scripture phrase,...which I'll look up in a minute is...'Underneath are the everlasting arms.' But the song is: 'Leaning, leaning, leaning on the arms of God my Savior'...and it just develops like that. The survivor...doesn't have anybody to lean on. You know,...everybody else is...dead on the trip and you come staggering out...because you have held on more tightly than anybody else. The survivor has nobody to lean on... and the experience of the Exercises was,...that when *really* pushed ...the survivor pushes himself more than anyone else pushes him,... *except* that he gets into...behaviors that invite other people to push him. And the Exercises helped me to see...that God is *there*....Not to catch me,...not just as kind of a safety net,...not to catch me when I make mistakes,...but holding me up...at *all* times...when I'm doing good stuff,...holding me up...and being glad of that. When I'm being stupid,...holding me up...and saying,...'relax, you don't have to do this.' And when I'm being just...just an utter jerk,...laughing at me and helping me to see...that I don't need to do that. But, I think,...yeah, it *really* is...really is....I wanted to get into how it is that the Spirit becomes a well of water gushing up...within the person. And it *does* that,...but it is very clear... for me...that that comes *after* the experience of...the everlasting arms. That before...before the Spirit enters me and...gushes up... as a spring of water,...I find myself emptied and exhausted,...and *resting* on these everlasting arms. And once I'm able to...to let go of the need to generate out of myself,...energy for the survival of the universe,...*then* the spring of water...begins to flow."

John: "The...not needing to protect people from experiencing life ...and the realization that you will always carry some pain about your first wife's death...and missing her,...and the realization... that God is in the ordinary...that that tasting this is not debilitating,

...how does that affect (when you look to the future)...how does that affect the way you think and feel about the future?"

Emmett: "I think that there is a certainty now...that God will... take care of me. That there's a lot that *I* don't have to do...about the future. And it will be clearest...as time goes on. The problem is the danger of falling into quietism...at this point...having been such a driven person...such a survivor,...such a stretched-out person,...that I could fall back and become flabby and...not work hard enough...not try hard enough...to be open and to be available. But, I think, in general,...I'm confident that the future that God has...is a future...is a future with hope. And...that He is doing better things than I can desire or pray for. The future may be to stay here in this parish for another twenty years. The future may be to go someplace else. At this point,...I *think* it true to say... that I'm fairly indifferent to that. There is a part of me...that I own that's ambitious and that would like to be in a bigger place. And I own that. I say,...'Okay, that's the truth...and that's part of me.' But I don't have to be driven by that....And I won't be unhappy ...if that doesn't happen. There's another part that would *like* to be the kind of person that stays at one place forever...and just disappear...into the life of the people. And there's a certain romanticism about that too,...that I'm aware of. So, where I am *now* is...I'm aware of both of these sides and...and *God* is going to make the decision about...which direction I go in...and will no doubt have ...places to correct and things to improve on...as they go."

John: "I'd like to ask...before we go into the litany of the before-and-after questions, if...in your experience of the Exercises,...if you experienced Jesus' presence *healing* you in anyway? And, if not that's fine. Everyone has different categories of how they understand this. So the question succinctly put is,...Jesus is often seen in the Scriptures healing people...Did you experience Jesus' healing graces?"

Emmett: "I think, yes. And it's interesting that you should mention that because I was writing an article for our parish magazine about healing...just recently...and the connection of healing and forgiveness came up,...Because we now are very nervous about... the connection of sin and sickness. But if you look at it in the positive,...the connection of healing and forgiveness is pretty clear.

So, without making any kind of one-to-one correspondences about sin making...particular sins giving particular sicknesses,...it's *very* true...that forgiveness is healing...and that healing involves forgiveness. So I experienced Jesus...forgiving me...for my failures, ...but not just for my failures...but for my unwillingness to admit to failures,...for my defensiveness,...Forgiving me and healing me of...the need to do it all on my own. There's this wonderful poem of Walt Whitman's called 'A Noiseless Patient Spider.' And it goes:

> A noiseless patient spider spins out
> filament, filament, filament out of himself.

"And that's a real image of me,...spinning this all out of my own gut. And I experienced the *beginning* of...a knowledge that God doesn't need me to do that...as much as I have done. That God is not asking me to spin...myself out. That God is giving me...life to share...rather than survival to wring from a rag. And so, I would say, yes. A lot of sense of healing,...and acceptance of self. Me as no better than I am. Me as somebody that God can use *with* my failings, *with* my compulsions, *with* my drivenness,...but to also let me be a little bit less driven...as time goes on."

John: "Emmett, I'm going to ask you that litany of before-and-after questions...and they all don't have to be answered. It's from the worksheet 'The Inner Heart of My Faith.' And the first question... that focuses the heart is, What would you say was your philosophy of life before the Spiritual Exercises,...and what is it like now in the present?"

Emmett: "Can I also do during and after? And this is interesting because this has become more clear. I think, before,...that *survival* was clearly my philosophy of life,...that survival was my task... from childhood on. And that in order to survive I *used* friends, I *used* women...my relationships with women with children. My children were *proof.* I remember by mother saying, when Nathaniel was born,...'Well you've finally done what you needed to do.' And so, you know,...that's built into our culture. During...the relatedness to God began to be more important than survival...and the realizing that *real* survival, *genuine* continuing in existence to eternal life ...has nothing to do with what I do to survive,...but has everything to do with God's wanting to be related to me. And, again,...the relationship was with Jesus, with Gerry, with my wife Anne and with my children. And in postretreat,...the sense that there is a world... out there...and I have a part in it. I don't have to *swallow* it. I don't have to defend myself from it. I don't have to protect anybody else from it. There is a *whole* universe...a whole world of reality...and that I have a place in it that is uniquely mine because God gave it to me. I didn't have to steal it or fight for it...or run away with it. God put me in it...and it's *my* place in the world."

John: "Thank you! Emmett...what was your greatest fear or anxiety before the Exercises and what is it now? Before, during, after,... however you would like to answer."

Emmett: "Well,...the *formal* intent...of undergoing the Exercises was to discern...to try to discern God's will around a vow of nonviolence...and trying to live a life of nonviolence...and what made it so...so real,...was the explosion of violence at the level where *I* lived in the parish...in my life...as it got closer and closer to this. It's so easy to think of Gandhi and Martin Luther King. It's not easy to be them, I'm sure. But it's easy to *think* of them as the nonviolent people. But to try to figure out how somebody like you or *I*...lives a life of nonviolence...there's not a lot of precedence for that...besides Jesus, I suppose. But...we think of it in a historical world... on the world scene...as big stuff. And Dick McSorely said to me... when I went to see him...a couple of years ago,...'You gotta live it out in your own life....You gotta live it out in your parish and your family.' And for *that*, there are no books written. You know,... we've got to write our own book. So,...the greatest fear or anxiety for *me*...was around violence. Both of my potentially being a victim of violence,...but much more...of my being a perpetrator of violence,...the violence that's in me that I know. I grew up in a violent culture. I remember a *profound* experience...in this journey for me ...was when I was about ten years old.......My grandfather told me he was going to bloody my face if I didn't do something. And I picked up a baseball bat and I said,...'Take another step and I'll kill you.' And I meant it. And it worked. So that violence is a pattern, is a part of my survival. I will *kill* in order to continue to exist...and to know that I didn't want to do that. So violence...and the sense that one of two things,...if confrontation and conflict come to a certain point, either I will explode into a million pieces and stop existing or

you will. And neither of those is an acceptable way of dealing with
conflict. So, ... to find a way where conflict, ... where violence is not
totally absorbing or destructive ... was part of what I was seeking.
During the Exercises I had the feeling that ... I wouldn't be able to
cope with real troubles, ... that I was just devastated by the realities.
Not the fantasies of exploding ... or of cosmic violence, ... but the
realities of living day to day ... in the situation that I was. And ...
this continues. I have a note here that says, 'Yesterday I didn't have
enough time' ... and I felt in myself the ... (and it could be any yesterday ... some more than others).... And there are more days that are
not ... not as driven.... But I let too many things be on my plate and
I go from one to the other ... sort of chasing my tail to catch up and
not getting it all done. And *I've* got to do it ... because, of course,
... nobody else can. There's a certain ease about that ... but it's not
achieved yet."

John: "Continuing with this litany of before-and-after questions, ...
What would you say was your greatest experience of joy or gratitude
before making the retreat ... and ... what is that now?"

Emmett: "I think ... bear in mind that before the retreat is about
fifty-two years ... and after is only two! But I've got down five words.
One was reading. All of my life it was a way into a world ... greater
than the world that I lived in. It was a power. An ability to ... sometimes ... sometimes I felt like Shakespeare and Dante and Aquinas
were closer friends than Johnny Jones on the street corner. Shakespeare and Dante and Aquinas are something that I can control ...
and Johnny Jones on the street corner ... had his own will and his
own mind.... I may not be as smart as Aquinas, but ... but I can
close the book. And so you can *manipulate* that past, ... you can manipulate what you read. Sex for me was ... an experience of authentic
life of ecstasy ... fatherhood. I was present when Nathaniel was born
... and we got to the hospital with twenty minutes to spare ... and
we had this list of names ... girl and boy. And Nathaniel wasn't on
them. He came out and then ... then the placenta came out ... and as
you may know there ... are two sides to it; one of which is a beautiful jewel-like thing and the other is just bloody flesh, you know,
bloody tissue. And this jewel was there and it was just *gorgeous* and
he was gorgeous ... and I thought, well, ... I've done this thing....
We didn't want to know whether it was a boy or girl, if they could
tell us ... because we felt quite clear that we were going to take what-

ever we got and we are *very* happy that our second child Sarah is a girl. It's nice to have both. So I hadn't had a whole...a great deal of this male stuff about wanting a son,...but my goodness... it was nice when he was born. It really felt *good* to...see a son... and like, you know,...maybe I can do for him...some of the stuff that wasn't done for me? It is an opportunity. And darkness,...the darkness is an old friend...as the song goes,...'I've always lived in this desert,...the desert and the darkness are places where I can go...when I need to....And, it's good to be.' And in the Exercises ...*light* came to be dominant. The idea of friendship,...I began to have an idea that friendship with God was what it was all about... in...1987...when I left Boston and came here. And...certainly this parish...in its first five years...taught me how difficult that friendship could be. And the last two years...it's been teaching me how wonderful it can be. With *friendship* coming to dominate everything in the Exercises,...That sense of friendship with Jesus...friendship with myself, friendship with the Father...this friendship. In the future...since the Exercises...I've taken up the guitar. I've taken up music. I've become...able to touch that part of myself. The desert is a living, blossoming place...at this point. In *fact*, the desert is one of the most beautiful, colorful places in the world. And Keeble's image...in the hymn of 'The Trivial Round, The Common Task'...what's *new* every morning is...is *everything* in life. And that...that the life to be lived *today*...is more important than *all* the future. And...and is the opportunity for the redemption of *all* the past. So, that's...*every day*...(I feel like I'm a recovering alcoholic)...I have only to live today. Today is the day that I have to offer to God. Today is the day that I have to live with God. And...if I do that, that's all He asks. And that's enough. And I can do it better and worse...but He loves me enough...to give me today."

John: "Wow, powerful stuff!...What was your greatest experience of sorrow before the Exercises...during...after?"

Emmett: "Certainly the death of my first wife was an *enormous* focus...of...sorrow. I think though, that there was a lot of sorrow...in my early life...that I never touched...that I never let myself feel. And *that* sorrow,...when she was sick, and when she was dying, and when she died,...really opened all that up...affected all that. And for a long time I had to just hide from it. It

was just too much. That was the greatest experience of sorrow...
before. During,...letting go of my self-image as the perfect priest,
as the one who could do everything. And I did this...I still work
about a sixty-hour week. And I did this thing because people wanted
to know what I did with my time. And I made out this list...and
people looked at it and they said,...'You must be crazy....When
do you spend time with your family?...When do you sleep?' And
to realize that that doesn't do any good for anybody,...That that's
compulsive behavior. That's craziness. Since then,...my experience
of sorrow...has been...in a couple of disappointments for myself
...where I have let myself be able to feel the disappointment...and
not be devastated by it. But more importantly...the experience of
other people's pain...as something which will not absorb me,...
but that *I* can be present to...and useful to,...but I do *feel* that
sorrow. You know,...I think...you probably experienced it in similar ways. That's *part* of the priestly vocation....We do *take on* and
we carry others' pains and sorrows. But we don't have to carry the
others. There's this wonderful thing in the Psalter...in an earlier
translation...'No man can give his life for another...or make a
ransom to God for him...so that he must let that alone *forever.*'
It's a wonderful thing! And yet, we *are* called to bear one another's
burdens...and we *can* bear one another's burdens. And so,...that's
an experience of sorrow...that is...*fruitful*...for me...since the
Exercises."

John: "Differentiations!...You said earlier, that we write our own
book...Well, you're doing it right here. What was your greatest
heartfelt desire?...(I keep using that word "heartfelt" because of
its evocative nature, you know...sort of thinking and feeling all in
one)...What was your greatest heartfelt desire before the retreat...
during...after?"

Emmett: "Well,...bearing in mind that before the retreat is fifty-two
years,...I think,...(and I certainly wouldn't have said it this way)
...but I think my greatest heartfelt desire was...to come to love and
accept myself...before the retreat. And I think that that happened,
...that because...I *finally* became persuaded of what God's been
trying to persuade me of for fifty-two years...and is still trying to
persuade me of...that He does love and accept me. That I could...
love myself. And I do."

John: "This is related to what you just said.... How did you regard yourself before making the Spiritual Exercises? How do you regard yourself now in the present?"

Emmett: "Well, I think I regarded myself as... as essentially a pretty unworthy son,... a son,... but an unworthy son. And the difference is... I don't think of myself as a worthy son,... but I know myself to be a loved son. So that, I think that,... it's as if the *categories* of worthy/unworthy have become less important... and left. I'm sure they're not gone... altogether yet. But it's become less important. I don't wake up every day... and say,... 'What a miserable sot I am, ... I'm an unworthy son... and no more worthy to be called Your son.' I wake up some days and... and just go about the business of being His son. Other days I wake up and feel unworthy. And every now and then I wake up and feel... like He didn't make a bad investment!"

John: "And the last question in the litany is,... What was your image of God... and your experience of God's regard like... before the retreat? And what is your image of God like now (if there's one particular thing that stands out)... and your experience of God's regard for you now?"

Emmett: "This is a really clear one. That for *many,* many years... I was one of those people who preferred the term "God." That God was my... (not Father because that was too intimate)... but *God*... was my preferred icon of the Lord... for relating to Him. In the Exercises, I was *compelled* to encounter Jesus: Jesus in His Godhead, Jesus in His Sonship, Jesus in His friendship with me, Jesus in His challenge to me. And, *afterward* it's been more and more... a relation to the Spirit... and to this spring of water gushing up... with the new believer's heart. Then I think it's still *crucial* that there is still something outside myself... (the everlasting arms... the Creator ... the Father... Jesus).... But, given that,... that given the security in resting on those everlasting arms,... that now... *now* the Spirit is welling up more and more from within. Now, it's more of an interior thing... for me."

John: "And in summary,... How would you describe what happened to you, in an overarching way? It's such a beautiful story that you just told in specific detail. If someone came up to you,... a parishioner or a fellow priest,... and said, 'Well... what is the experience of the Spiritual Exercises like,... What did it do for you?' In a nutshell summary,... what would you say?"

Emmett: "This *really* is new,... because after we talked awhile ago, I realized that I had... it was the first time that I had sat down and thought this extensively about the Exercises and learned... and seen what the effect had been. I mean I finished the Exercises and carried on with life. What it was for me, was a... deepening of conversion, ...a making real... of what I had always believed... and tried to practice. But like giving it to me... on a platter,... it was *given* that it was real. I began to trust my experience... more than I had ever done before... my experience of God, my experience of Jesus, my experience of the Spirit, my experience of the church, my experience of myself, my experience of the people I love, my family, my parish. It's real! And there's not a... an abyss between me and my experience,... me and the world... that I experience. That abyss was... was *closed* in some way. I think it can open up from time to time,... but it's been bridged."

Summary

Emmett entered into the experience of the Spiritual Exercises out of an undergirding desire to grow in self-acceptance. A "formal intent" within him grew out of this desire, namely, the intent to discern whether or not God was calling Emmett to take a vow of nonviolence. Through the gentle mediation of his spiritual director, Emmett was invited and enabled to trust God's leadings. The retreat began amid serious experiential conflicts both internal and external. His multicultural parish was experiencing racial strife, while within Emmett a destructive survival mode was operating in his ministerial heart. The past had created learned patterns of self-sufficient survival. He came to realize that these felt patterns of strength were "resistances" closing him off and keeping him from relating to God, self, and the world at large. They could be unlearned.

Healing grace is experienced around the central conflict within Emmett's heart, the conflict of unrelated affective movements attached to failures and personal inadequacies. Emmett came to delight in his humanity with all its mixed motives, dysfunctions, and ordinariness. Surprised by God's love when he brought his inner feelings to prayer, Emmett experienced "enormous acceptance" from God as

Father. His prayer is explicitly Trinitarian. As Emmett trusts God specifically as Father with his human flaws, Emmett tastes sonship and feels compelled to be with Jesus as friend and brother. The Spirit is experienced as an indwelling spring or font of flowing energy whenever Emmett feels most limited (e.g., the inability to prevent his first wife's dying). So deep is this Trinitarian relational friendship that it overrides and shapes all of his other relationships. From within Emmett this divine intimacy re-creates whole new sets of friendship, a felt solidarity with others, a new ability to appreciate nature and play music, and, most remarkably, the ability to befriend conflicts with a nonviolent heart.

Perfectionism is partially winnowed away from Emmett's experience in day-to-day life. The delusion that he needs to be purer or better than others as a priest begins to depart. Compulsions of overresponsibility, protecting others from the real pains of life are addressed by Jesus' Spirit and partially healed. Deep relief occurs from well-hidden, burdensome sorrows left over from his wife's death. The Holy Spirit fosters self-forgiveness within Emmett, teaching him that the world is already redeemed. If he will continue to embrace the present with all of its flaws and ordinariness, confidence in the future and redeeming grace are accessible for interior tasting. Exercising interpersonal conversation within the Trinity brings about unitive experiences of healing grace for Emmett. He experiences interior and exterior conflicts merging within a new heart. This new heart remains extra aware of being held and cared for amid conflict and experiences no separation between the world and his personal faith.

In between the lines of Emmett's felt consolations lie patterns of persistent darkness deserving attention informing pastoral diagnosticians. Emmett admittedly feels awake to the struggle within of further accepting himself as totally loved by God. He carries a real need to be healed of perfectionism resulting in an overly protective heartfelt posture, specifically regarding relationships with women. Emmett has also received feedback from parishioners advising him that they see him as overextended in his pastoral work. He agrees. Emmett's sixty-hour work week provides evidence of what he names as "compulsive behavior...craziness."

An interior strain exists in Emmett between experiencing God's love, yielding to graced self-acceptance amid a flawed human nature, and the actual destructiveness of his drive for perfection. This strain remains very much alive in Emmett's walk with experiencing

Jesus in "his Godhead, Sonship, and Friendship." Guideline #321 in Ignatius's teachings for discerning hearts growing in a capacity for freedom from disordered affections is illustrated in Emmett's situation. Emmett will need to cultivate an attitude of patience around his experiences of persistent desolation. This will aid him in mitigating afflictions which these desolations signify. He has described several of his experiences of God's healing consolations as "beginnings." And this needs to be acknowledged as time and grace restore Emmett's personality in Christ, in his evolving Trinity-oriented relationships.

The art of spiritual direction should actively attend to encouraging Emmett to obediently return to resting in and being with those interior movements of consolation that are presently multiplying his heart's felt faith and hope. The experience of sharing God's laughter in the face of destructive perfectionism regularly unburdens Emmett from a false and unhealthy activism in ministry.

Emmett needs to be held accountable, firmly but gently in spiritual direction, to reflecting upon the quality of his response with this profoundly consoling movement of laughter being given by Jesus' Spirit. Otherwise he may spin out of the very inner relating that heals compulsive living.

Time will tell the true story, if Emmett remains faithful, permitting himself to receive God's steadfast love. But the mystery of reverencing Emmett's patterns of desolation may reveal a need for him to revisit what he concluded to be heartfelt confirmations of a desire to take a public vow of nonviolence. A cautious questioning of Emmett's conclusion may discover elements of personal compulsion at work, the vow becoming a type of forced capping of inner rages and angers left over from a violent upbringing. Paradoxically, if this is the case, a hidden form of violence minimizing Emmett's everyday receiving of even more healing from the divine physician would have transpired in the form of a religious vow.

The art of Ignatian spiritual direction requires comfort with ambiguities, and it depends, in part, upon open-ended prudent skepticism. As stated in Guideline #333, the evil spirit should be suspected to attempt to twist good beginnings toward evil directions, possibly even to an evil end. There need be no fear or anxiety for Emmett. In time, the fruits of the Holy Spirit or their absence will illuminate his faith journey. And "underneath are God's everlasting arms." The simple question remains about whether or not Emmett's conclusion about what he perceived to be God's calling to take this vow was based in the truth which ultimately sets hearts free (John 8:31–32).

General Questions for Personal Reflection

1. Do you let yourself admit failures and personal inadequacies? After acknowledging a few and taking your inner heart's feelings to Jesus in prayer, describe the experience of relating with Jesus' Spirit.

2. Name a conflict that has been (or is being) played out inside of you. How is God's reconciling presence experienced as leading you in the middle of that conflict?

Specific Practicum Questions for Spiritual Directors

1. In the ministry of spiritual direction explain what is evoked in your experience as "mediator" of God's grace for the directee.

2. Utilizing the "Guidelines for the Discernment of Spirits" (Appendix I), render a pastoral diagnosis for Emmett. Name the guidelines you see operating in the patterns of his story.

Chapter Three

MELISSA'S EXPERIENCE OF HEALING PRAYER

Profile

Melissa, age thirty-eight, is single, Roman Catholic, lives and works as part of our economic middle class, and grew up in an Irish-American family. She enjoys employment as a liturgical musician and spiritual director in university campus ministries. Melissa received a master's degree in Spiritual Theology after following an inner sense of call to pursue studies that would simultaneously deepen her personal relationships in faith while opening up new dimensions of her career services. Following the traditional "retreat house" format of the Spiritual Exercises, Melissa prays about an hour a day. She frequently uses the "Examination of Consciousness" and receives Christ's eucharistic presence daily. Melissa describes the Spiritual Exercises as "a life-changing, felt-living reality,...a being loved and cared for by God,...washed in mercy at the core."

Interview with Melissa

John: "This is Melissa's conversational interview about the Spiritual Exercises...and what her experience is like now having made that. So Melissa the first question that I'd like you to address is...simply: 'What was the greatest or one of the greatest experiences of God's love that you experienced while making the Exercises?'"

Melissa: "I think the deepest experience for me was being at Mary's breast and being nursed by her,...an experience of receiving the milk, which is a symbol of being taken care of by God...and continues to be a major point,...like a central focus point for me in

54

self and relationships...and the whole posture of how I am in the world."

John: "Can you describe how it happened that you had this experience of drinking milk at Mary's breast? In other words, if you were (without being analytical)...if you were listening to this transcription...could you describe for someone...how you got to that experience,...and a little bit more about what it was like."

Melissa: "I don't remember the exact meditation where it happened, ...but I know it was in the stories and reflections of Jesus' life... and I believe it was in meditating on Jesus being at Mary's breast in the infancy narratives...and in that...experiencing first holding Jesus...and then Mary's desire to hold me and to nurse me. And it just happened...it kind of unfolded in reflecting on the readings... and letting my own imagination kind of take it where it would."

John: "Can you say more about what the experience was like and what you felt?"

Melissa: "The experience was of the freedom of being a child,...of feeling that raw and vulnerable and dependent. And I felt that kind of abandonment in it,...the freedom of it, the lack of responsibility. ...I received great tenderness in it,...a sense of my deepest needs being filled,...Of being able to be raw,...being able to be naked,... being childlike...and just receiving the milk and receiving the nourishment. And I felt a great sense of...'being taken care of'...are the words that keep coming back to me. It's a...nurturing in places of pain and of hurt that were not able to be nurtured in concrete experiences. And deep places within myself...of pains and hurts and fears and anxieties...where I receive the milk...it's a...felt experience of acceptance...of being loved and of feeling joy in who I am, ...in being lovable,...that the false fears fall away and I just feel the acceptance."

John: "Can you say what any of those fears and anxieties were that fell away...fall away?"

Melissa: "One of the deep fears for me is...fear of abandonment... and that comes out of my own childhood experience of my mother being ill,...and both of my parents being much older, and the fear they were going to die when I was little...because they were so much older and there was so much sickness in the family. And I felt a sense of a need to care for them. So, I felt adult responsibility as a child...and the fear was, they're going to go away...and the deeper fears are...that I did something to cause this...or that somehow I should be able to make them better, or heal them, or alleviate the suffering...somehow. So that the deepest fears are of abandonment, ...of being the one to cause pain,...just by who I am,...of hurting or not being able to help or to heal. And the healing of that is... a freedom from that,...a freedom from a sense of responsibility to have to take care of others. And the deepest healing,...being taken care of in it...of receiving milk. It's the tangible quality of tasting and feeling nourishment happening...in the rawness and the messiness...in watching suffering or watching people I love...die even. Or, in ministry...of wanting to help others or to pour out my life for them. The healing there is...God loving me and feeding me... and nourishing me...in the midst of being called to ministry."

John: "So how has your ministry toward others changed...as a result of this experience? How do you experience ministry, now?"

Melissa: "Well,...that's a good question. Being at Mary's breast... and receiving the milk is the place of decisions...and the place of reality for me. So,...ministry changes...because my decisions are made there. And who I am is in that. The decisions are different... because...I'm not making decisions out of a false sense of...'I have to take care of'...or 'I have to be the one to heal'...or 'I have to be the one to save.' It doesn't come out of that false sense...that... the decisions come out of the freedom of abandonment...of abandonment to God's care and the reality of *God* taking care of the world,...of all things being in Him. So,...the decisions are different. What I might do...that might seem really wonderful in terms of hours and hours of work or trying to help all of these people, etc., etc.,...could often in fact...be self-destructive,...could be not what God wills, not God's desires for me,...not the way that God loves me,...coming out of His love for me. So it changes priorities ...and the gift of being loved,...of being nurtured, deepens my own desire for God. Intimacy with God,...understanding of God's heart, of God's will...and deepens my own desire for the more, the magis ...for being with Him in more intimate places. So that as I'm fed at the most intimate places within myself,...there's a growing desire in me...concretely...to share that with others. And to be,...like to make choices that...chose the more intimate places in people's lives...or the deeper...and to experience joy,...to experience being nurtured *in* the ministry...allows me to walk more deeply into Jesus' ministry."

John: "How is it that you know...that being at Mary's breast and being nourished...in that core identity?...How do you know that that is God's Spirit speaking to you...and not an illusion,...to rationalize doing less in ministry? You can see how someone might see doing less...as a form of selfishness...and then kind of rationalizing it. But...you seem very confident that this is your core identity in God...in this nursing, this nourishment,...where you say all your needs are being experientially met or attended to. How do you know that that's God's Spirit and not an illusion?"

Melissa: "I think it's the fruits. I experience healing,...healing of pain,...of self-doubts and self-images,...like there's a freedom,...like a greater freedom...inside myself,...so that, I experience myself differently,...like working toward more of the wholeness,...more of what it means to be human, what it means to be a human person,...the same kind of process that you would go through in psychological counseling. So that there's a much stronger image of self,...felt acceptance of self at core hurts and mistakes,...A falling away of a lot of compulsions,...A freedom to take risks in different things,...Of decisions to do harder things,...A shift in relationships where I can feel and see patterns that aren't good or relationships that are mixed,...where I have healthier relationships, and also the development of more intimate relationships."

John: "You've said so much. That's so full. Let's stop and let's try to get very specific. I mean you already are specific,...but let's try to get more specific. Could you describe your experience of the healing of compulsions? Could you name some of the inner compulsions that have been...or are being touched? Could you name some of the relationships which have changed? And I forget the third thing that you mentioned...besides the compulsions and relationships. Let's just go with those."

Melissa: "Let me start with relationships. One set is my family... and part of it is/was...a real felt sense of responsibility in my family...to take care of them. And recently there was a situation with my brother and sister-in-law and my nieces...of real alienation...

with both of my nieces, and accusations against some of the family members... in deeply painful situations,... and my really getting caught in that,... and my trying to appease both sides... and heal... and seeing a false sense of self in that,... that I didn't have to take care of or mediate. A greater freedom to let it be, to let the difficulty speak,... the pain speak for itself. And so there's a shifting... in freedom in the relationships... just to let them work it out. And in my friendships,... there was one relationship in particular with a friend, Pete, who I saw on retreat as really being annihilation for me, ... where it was a series of lots of conversations... where I was just trying to take care of him,... and really denying myself,... like who I was in the relationship,... like almost losing my sense of self with him. So that... it wasn't *mutual* friendship and I could see that,... and a couple other relationships, too,... that I struggled with. That there was a lot of pain with,... Sarah in particular, and two college friends. And in them... an experience of feeling that they didn't quite understand me... and accept me, or what I believed in or who I was, ... that I was still trying to live up to some kind of image... or afraid to let it go. And then affirmation of some of the closest friends that I have... who affirm who I am, *in faith*,... who affirm who I am at my deepest core. And where that's just grown, even to a deeper sense of intimacy with these people.

"The compulsions,... the compulsion *to do*, I think,... is the top one. I always have to be doing something. I have to be doing something for others. To do something for myself is selfish... and feels wrong. Probably a compulsion to be very self-critical... and to want perfectionism within myself.... So a real sense that,... that if there's mistakes or sin or inadequacies (things that I can't do — limitations) that often it gets internalized... that this is me. This is core hurting me... or sense of shame in that. And the healing,... the process that continues to unfold,... but which took part largely at the core in retreat was first one about doing,... really feeling God is inviting me to vacation,... That vacation is a part of *every day*,... which feels selfish at times. But that, that's the truth of it. That's the reality of who I am in God. And an experience of knowing *when* there's some form of vacation... even if it's time for prayer... or for good conversation with people, or exercise or whatever.... When that's an element, the decisions are better. The productivity is even better... in a sense of quality of time with people,... or quality of decision making. And the sense of self is fuller, healed,... so that the self-doubts and the self-criticism and the demands...are not out of compulsion. There's much more gentleness with myself,...a gentleness of freedom to be ...and I think a gentleness with other people,...so that I'm much less hyper about stuff and much better able...to rest in being who I am."

John: "Could you say more about what the primary experience of nursing at Mary's breast is like,...because I'm asking you to go back to that for what is probably an obvious reason....I mean,... you just explained so much of what seems to come out of that core identity,...or what does come out of that core identity. So, it would really be helpful,...if you could for yourself...and for others, explain the experience. Again,...not analyzing...but just descriptively naming experiences and,...Can you just say more about what is in that experience?"

Melissa: "What's in it is feeling God's love,...feeling being fed at the places of deepest pain,...of being nursed...in rawness, like in the messiest parts of myself....in the places I don't easily share with other people...or even admit to in myself,...And that's where God is. That's where God...it's not even just that He's present, but it's the image of milk,...of it being life source,...like being engaged, being evoked,...something dynamic...that continues to unfold...and stirs up creativity in me...and my own desire to nurse,...you know, to pour out my milk...to share with others. It's a sense of receiving, of fullness, of acceptance,...of peace in fear,...with the image of *resting* in...and being held and embraced,...abandonment."

John: "I take it that this image is still with you?"

Melissa: "Very much so...very much so."

John: "How is it still with you?"

Melissa: "It's a core experience. In prayer, it's the place I return to, ...as a posture for prayer. In decision making,...this is the place where I make my decisions now,...Where I know that the best decision,...the truest decisions for myself...and also God's will...is found here. So that the times when...I'm too restless to be in Mary's arms or at Mary's breasts receiving...and off doing and fixing,... I'm usually making decisions out of compulsions and out of...my own sense that I have to get this done or I have to do this. When I'm vulnerable enough to receive...then the decisions come out of a deeper place of self...and ultimately...are decisions that are the more...that are God's will,...and I think that more deeply touch and affect people's lives...and I can see that...and people have said that in me,...to notice it in me. There's a deeper peace. People have commented that I just seem much more happy...and content. And I feel a richness,...like a deeper richness in the quality of the days. And in fear,...in moments of anxiety and fear,...this is a place of comfort. This is the place where...the fears are alleviated,...where I can find comfort...and where I can discern,...where I can see what's going on in my life,...where I get a better sense of clarity ...of all the mixture of things that are going on for me."

John: "Let's try to shift gears a little bit. And, it's a question about resistance. Here's the core image that unfolded...as you said... through praying with Scripture in the retreat. How do you experience resistance to receiving? And,...if you can...describe how you experience that most poignantly?"

Melissa: "Two images....One is again...being at Mary's breast... and either gagging on the milk,...like feeling that I can't take it in or...running away,...like I have too much to do. It's almost like a child...wanting to run out and play,...and just being too active so that I can't rest. And the other experience, too, in the same way is... being with God, letting God love me,...being embraced by God or ...letting God make love to me...and a sense of restlessness in that, ...a sense of...being afraid to be that vulnerable....And in resistance...I walk away from it. I leave Mary's arms. I walk away from the embrace of God...feeling unworthy to be there,...feeling that I need to do something...in order to be there...or I need to earn God's love in some way. And what I've just, you know,...come to see...through retreat and after it...is that a lot of the compulsiveness of *doing*...is really feeling that I need to do...in order to...let God love me. That it's not possible for God to love me...in the rawness,...as a child...receiving. My resistance is,...when it feels like it's selfish. I feel selfishness. I feel like this is selfish to be...at Mary's breast...or to let God hold me. I feel it's selfish not to do more, ...like in terms of physical activity, concrete activity,...that to take vacation is selfish...and it feels like that's really true, like it should be true,...that to take vacation in the middle of a day is selfish. If I'm really ministering...then...I'm not going to take vacation in the middle of a day. But again and again and again,...I experience it as resistance... and most poignantly... that on retreat that the mode *vacation*... was part of every day... and came up again and again and again and again,... and that... that God was calling me to experience vacation,... which felt like a contradiction to me... at the time."

John: "Could you say any more about what the gagging feels like ... and how you sinned by saying yes to the gagging? It's a different understanding of sin than most people carry,... but I'm equating resistance with sin here. In other words,... not participating where there is felt nourishment,... not letting yourself be part of where there is nourishment and life."

Melissa: "The gagging feels like choking,... like I can't take it in. The image is like... my throat is closing. I can't swallow,... so I experience the gagging as,... it's fear,... like where the fear closes off... or restlessness. I can't stay in Mary's arms. I have to go *do*. Let me go over here and finish this,... then I'll come back. So, what I experience is my own shame surfacing,... my own sense of unworthiness, ...sinfulness,... poverty... and the fear in that... and the false sense of Mary rejecting me in that... or God rejecting me in that. So that the sin is... not letting God love me in that. It's not that I'm not sinful, it's not that I'm not weak, it's a call to embrace that more,... like a call to let God love me in that more,... a call to receive the milk in that. Again, the image of being... a child, of being naked... and of being humble enough,... simple enough,... to let God take care of me... in all the messiness of that."

John: "You mentioned messiness a number of times. Could you say a little bit more about... what you experience as messy in yourself? ... Where you experience God's love."

Melissa: "I think the first place of messiness is... what I feel as imperfection. Again, going back to the inability to heal... to do for others. And in myself... a sense of shame... of core shame... at who I am,... at the imperfection of who I am,... of the rawness,... that there is sin, that there are mistakes,... that I don't do it right,... that I can never do enough in the eyes of others or in the eyes of myself... in the sense of... feeling limitations and vulnerabilities. And the messiness is, you know,... concrete examples of times in my life when I've made mistakes and I've been sinful and I've walked away from God,... where I've lost a sense of self in relationships,... where even my vision of caring for others is too narrow, or my sense of justice is not broad enough,... or my sense of responsibility for sin or for evil in the world is just not open enough. And I think the deepest part of it is... the messiness of where God is,... like not letting God heal,... of kind of what feels like blasphemy... or the unspeakable things to say to God... that I'm angry at Him for... my vulnerabilities, or for my weakness, or the fears that I might feel,... or why is something this way,... or just that He longs to love me... there... where it feels unlovable."

John: "Again shifting gears a little bit,... I'd like you to just relax ... and try to recall other experiences of God's presence with you, ... Mary's presence with you... during the retreat. There's this core identity of being nursed at Mary's breast... and you very fully described what that is like, what that was like... and what's come out of it. Just take the conversation where you would like it to go,... What else to remember in terms of poignant experiences of God's love... from the Exercises?"

Melissa: "A couple things are real poignant. One is... a feeling of being washed in Mercy... at my core self,... not just things that I did wrong... or something here or something there;... but core identity as being washed in Mercy. Being naked with God,... again, that kind of rawness,... vulnerability,... there's nothing that can't be said or revealed or shared,... and even an invitation to continually go more deeply into that.... So a sense of being naked... with God... and being loved in it. An experience of the two standards... of felt annihilation and felt freedom.... And the image for me is a sense that the annihilation is darkness... where I turn in on myself,... where I feel a lot of the self-doubts,... And it's isolation, alienation,... separation from... my best self, from others, from God.... And that's darkness."

John: "And what feelings accompany that darkness,... that experience of darkness?"

Melissa: "I feel isolated and alone. I feel bad about myself. I feel unable to share with others. It taps into a core sense of felt shame. Shame at who I am,... that I'm unlovable. And I feel powerless, ... powerless to do, to be present to others,... powerlessness in the world.... Not a sense of powerless in... in abandoning in a good

way,... but kind of chained... or blocked. A real sense of unfree-
dom,... that I'm bound by darkness.... And the sense that is, is
light,... like radiance. It's color. It's a broad horizon,... where I feel
loved even in imperfection.... I feel loved... and called to know
God's delight in me,... to know... how God loves and cares for me,
... to know the reality of my identity in God... so that the sunset is
... an experience of self, in the midst of creation,... kind of this...
broad expanse,... I don't know, a sense of wideness in the world,...
a sense of light and color and beauty... that is... the reality of God's
creation, that is felt interiorly within myself,... that is experiencing
joy... in sharing Jesus' ministry.

"And another significant place for me is... being at the cross
with Jesus. And the significance is the difference in the experience,
... where I could be at the cross. The cross has always been an
important place for me,... a symbol of self-emptying love for me.
The difference now is being taken care of at the cross, with Jesus.
A key place for me was Gethsemane,... where I felt... a real false
sense of what Gethsemane was.... And for me it was... feeling that
... precisely in the moment of trial,... the moment when things are
overwhelming and really powerful... that,... that's when abandonment occurs. And that in that sense of being alone and isolated is
where the trial is... or where the suffering and death occurs. And I
mean... just to realize just how false that is... in experiencing the
Trinity's love,... in knowing Jesus,... feeling the love of the Trinity
... in His own experience. And for me,... of being loved *in suffering*
... of God's love of Jesus' cross... as being symbolic of Him entering into suffering. So that my experience is His love,... feeling His
love... in the midst of difficulties, trials,... sharing and suffering,...
which takes the burden out of suffering,... and helps me to experience even... joy in suffering,... because of the intimacy of the place
inside of me... and the place inside of Jesus where we share."

John: "Is there anything more you can say about,... being taken care
of... at the cross?"

Melissa: "Well, it feels like... my initial reaction is... that this can't
be right. Again, the sense of... it's selfish... or it must be wrong.
But my experience in it is... feeling love,... feeling the awe of God's
love for me and for others, for the world.... So that it internalizes
redemption,... it internalizes Jesus' outpouring of love... as a felt
experience within me... to feel that love... and to know it, not only

with me and Jesus, but to know it as *reality*. And there's a point
of intimacy. The cross is ... for me ... is complete outpouring, ... like
there's nothing ... it's abandonment for me, ... self-emptying love, ...
so that there's not anything being held back. And the point of intimacy is my pouring myself out, ... the idea of the Suscipe ... of giving
God everything ... again and again and again, ... and Jesus pouring
everything out ... with this incredible understanding ... of unity, of
oneness, of intimacy, ... beyond my wildest imaginings, ... of joy, ...
fulfillment, ... fulfillment inside of self, fulfillment in relationship, ...
in relationship to Jesus, in intimacy to God, ... and fulfillment in
terms of the world, ... like of the image of kingdom for me, ... that
in this is the deepest experience of God's kingdom ... and that this
is God's will, ... kind of the fulfillment of the kingdom to be ... that
continues to unfold."

John: "Is there any shame in that experience?"

Melissa: "Do you mean, ... do I experience shame as I experience
Jesus' love?"

John: "I simply asked that question because before ... you mentioned being with Jesus in nakedness was ... inviting you ... to delve
more deeply into that reality and experience of love. And you had
mentioned before that there was some shame there. I was wonder-
ing if there was in the cross ... this experience of self-emptying and
kingdom ... any shame ... or if that was different?"

Melissa: "I don't think there is. I think it's different.... Yeah, ... it
is different ... because I'm caught up in Jesus, ... I'm caught up ...
in His love ... and the focus isn't on me, the focus is on Jesus, ... but
it's a dynamic of Jesus and I sharing, or Jesus entering into the world.
So I don't ... I'm not conscious of shame. I'm caught up in a different
dynamic."

John: "We're going to shift gears one last time ... and this has been
beautiful and very deep. What I'm going to do now is refer back
to the reflection worksheet, 'The Inner Heart of My Faith,' and I'm
just going to ask you to give brief answers ... before and after the
Spiritual Exercises type of questions. And if you can answer them,
great. And if not, ... and you want to leave them blank, ... that's fine,
too. But we'll use this as a wrap-up of our conversational interview.
So the first question is that one about your philosophy of life. Could

you briefly say what your philosophy of life was like... before the Spiritual Exercises... and contrast it to what it's like now,... after the Spiritual Exercises?"

Melissa: "Before was... a sense of giftedness, a sense of all is gift ... and that my basic posture was... kind of offering praise and thanksgiving to God... *for* creation itself,... and also a sense of... my posture as thanksgiving, liturgy being foundational,... and ministry as... being able to answer or take care of the needs of others, ... with a sense of ministry as being able to meet others' needs or do as much as I could for other people. After is,... there's vacation in every day,... a real sense of being loved and being taken care of in life,... and a change in God's love,... I mean a change in ministering, ... where it's a sense of being loved and taken care of *in* ministry,... that what I do or what I hope to do... comes out of a deeper sense of longing to... share in the more, to share... in the joy of being at the cross with Jesus,... but being taken care of in that, being loved in that,... which is greater freedom."

John: "A little bit more about the word "vacation."... Could you just say very succinctly,... a synonym for "vacation"... as you are using the word. When you say your philosophy of life is a little vacation in each day now,... what does that mean?"

Melissa: "Being taken care of."

John: "Thank you. The next question is, what was your greatest fear ... or what were your greatest fears before the Spiritual Exercises... and what is your greatest fear now after the Exercises?"

Melissa: "Before was fear of abandonment. Key,... absolutely key, ... fear of being left alone,... fear of abandonment by God,... abandonment by others in the vulnerabilities, in the rawness, in perfection,... in inability to do.

"Fears now,... there's some traces of it, but it's lessening. And... I think that there's more... of a sense of not wanting to walk away from God,... a real keen sense of *choice*... that God loves me so much that I have the freedom to choose... and to make decisions ... that either lead me more into His love and the reality of that... or lead me away from it,... so that the fears are... I don't know,... maybe it is fear of the Lord? I really haven't named it as that before, ... but not wanting to choose walking away from Him,... walking away from God,... walking away from being at the breast of Mary."

John: "In continuing our litany here, from the reflection sheet, what was your deepest experience of joy, of gratitude, before the Spiritual Exercises... and how about in the everyday... now?"

Melissa: "Before was a sense of God being present in suffering, a sense of resurrection,... a reality that there is resurrection in life, ... a lot of joy at relationships... at family and friends,... at experiences of faith,... of faith community,... of knowing that as my core identity,... of sharing in Jesus' ministry,... lots of pain of past sufferings,... and a sense of God saving me in times of my life that were difficult... and times where I would wander away,... times when I would walk away from God,... make decisions,... particularly one time in my life where I went through a really painful time in my job ... and in relationships... of feeling abandonment by family... of my mother having died,... of a significant relationship breaking up for me,... and feeling that I lost myself in it,... that I was so needy... that I would almost do anything to be with people,... to have intimacy in romantic relationships... or in personal friendships,... and a real sense of cynicism about the realities of life... of human brokenness,... of pain in the church,... disappointments of what was going on in the church or in the world,... Kind of a loss of idealism, ... and a real sense of God coming to me in that... and after deep pain,... but of God calling to work through that, or to come to a deeper understanding of... love in that."

John: "That was before the retreat?"

Melissa: "Right. That's all before."

John: "How about now after the retreat?"

Melissa: "After... the joy of being loved *in* the messiest parts of myself,... the joy of God wanting the deepest intimacy with me,... of feeling a different identity,... where I think I would have described myself as... kind of being independent and doing things on my own, ... that's the image I have. And now, I think, my identity as more of being spouse,... of being married to God,... in the sense of God being with me in... God longing,... the most romantic, idealized relationship with me... of sharing everything,... Of making decisions ... where it's God and I making decisions,... not that *I* have to make it... or the burden is on me. The burden isn't on me anymore. There's mutuality and respect,... and real joy at being called to walk with Jesus,...to minister with Him,...to share more deeply in His life...and in knowing the joy in suffering,...knowing the lack of burden in being at the cross...and experiencing love in that."

John: "Your deepest experience of sorrow...before the retreat and now? In some ways, you've already addressed that,...but perhaps you want to say something more? Take it wherever you'd like it to go."

Melissa: "Sorrow before is largely in...suffering within my family, particularly my mom,...both the death of my mom and my dad,... long bouts of suffering with both of them beforehand. Sorrow in the situation that I described earlier...of a loss of idealism and cynicism and felt loss of self in relationships,...sorrow in the family,...alienations that I've experienced recently. And sorrow and deep sadness at...kind of a posture of,...I don't know whether it's being hard on myself in the way I describe it,...not being able to do enough,... with a real...kind of sense of beating myself up. Of,...I can never do enough. I can never be enough. It's core...dissatisfaction or inability to accept weakness.

"Sorrow, now,...is *with* God, it's...sorrow at the times that I walk away from,...that I gag at Mary's breast,...sorrow when I can feel my own core sinfulness surface. Kind of my own pride,... my own desire for protection of myself,...which is not freedom,... which is not abandonment to God's care and God's love. Sorrow,... there's a difference in the sadness that I feel in the world...in not ...before it was focused on the pain I felt in people's sufferings,... pain at injustices. I think that it shifts to...sorrow at...the word that comes to me is 'greed.' I guess it's a posture of self-emptying,... The greed of economic structures or of...I seem to be much more focused on...structural things or...policies that will affect people or interior postures within people,...where they make decisions. So that the sadness or the sorrow is kind of an identity in...something parallel that happens inside of me,...where...there's a separation of suffering and pain. It's not so much that I want to fix the pain of people who are hurting...or in poverty or broken or in war,...as much as the sorrow is...in the structures or the ability of people to hurt each other...or to inflict suffering on others."

John: "Your way of regarding yourself before and after the retreat?"

Melissa: "Before,... prime image is caretaker. I regarded myself as the one who had to heal,... the one who had to bear the pain,... take on the suffering."

John: "And after?"

Melissa: "After,... the one who's cared for."

John: "What is your experience of how God regards you... before and after?"

Melissa: "Before,... God sees me walking with... a companion,... someone that He cares for and takes care of and,... but not in the same way. Kind of being present to... or being with... *in* suffering. But after is... God takes delight in me. God desires me. God thirsts for me. And God loves me so much to want to intimately share with me... and desires me to be spouse,... to share with Him in ministry. But it's to know joy... at the deepest level,... at the deepest points of intimate sharing in the cross and resurrection."

John: "Perhaps this is best gotten at through the image of you being with Jesus at Gethsemane,... or perhaps it's best gotten at through what you said was your great experience of God's love,... nursing at Mary's breast. But... the question to end with is simply,... What were your deepest desires before the retreat, and what do you find them to be now?"

Melissa: "My deepest desire before... was to know Jesus,... to be companion with Jesus. The image of walking with Jesus in the village,... with the people. My deepest desire was to give everything to Jesus... and to share with Him... in love and in ministry. And now, it's... to be with Him in love at the cross,... to experience the joy of being taken care of... at the deepest point of intimacy... in sharing in the cross and resurrection,... and even to know the joy of thanking God for rejections or for humiliations of pains. So, that it's... it comes out of a different place,... The image again... of being loved at the cross."

John: "What is the cross for you, specifically now,... or where do you experience being at the cross... most poignantly?"

Melissa: "I think it's... it's a combination of... the intimacy of God loving me in the deepest parts of myself,... the places where I've never expressed deep fears, deep anxieties,... ongoing, day-to-day experiences of that. And also,... an experience of... the shifts of relationships, the shifts of decision making,... where it's always choosing, hopefully... the more,... but choosing at the breast of Mary. So that it's being loved in those decisions that are often painful ... or often participate in Christ's suffering. But... where I know myself as being loved,... even in difficult decisions and in an intimate sense of sharing in ministry with others."

John: "In trying to explain to someone,... in a nutshell,... what your experiences of the Spiritual Exercises is like,... How would you describe them?... If someone just came up to you and said they were thinking of making the Exercises,... what would you say your experience was like?"

Melissa: "It's life changing, but not in the ways that I thought. It's not like a pinnacle experience, where... everything is wonderful... and it's this great high... and then everything changes,... Or, you know, ... I change dramatically as a person... or something like that. It's a deeper internal experience. It's life changing,... in that, for me it allows me to live in reality... and knowing reality as being loved by God,... and knowing reality as Jesus redeems us and comes into our world... and loves us so intimately that... redemption is there. With a real sense of being called to deep intimacy to share... with God... in this,... in this love and in the sense of... bringing the kingdom to fulfillment."

Summary

The foundational desire at work prior to and during Melissa's faith experience in the Spiritual Exercises was her desire to know Jesus. This desire met with God's desire "thirsting" for her! A spiritual marriage unfolded as Melissa prayed within scriptural images that mediated fundamental healing graces. She allowed herself to be held, nursed, and cared for in the poignantly consoling sexual image of Mary's breast. The interpenetration of this deepening grace, one of profoundly felt acceptance amid an inner messiness, dynamically carries Melissa to stand within the imagination of her heart at Calvary. Through conversing with Jesus' presence in the image of the cross, Melissa receives new inner freedom from compulsions and burdens, as well as a new inner freedom to serve in ministry by meaningfully "suffering-with-Jesus."

Inner healings realized include dramatic removals of the fear of being abandoned and of her overly responsible need to care for others. Both are attributable to Melissa's having taken on adult responsibilities for her sickly parents as a child. A new ministerial posture results. Melissa is more able to see relationships for what they really are in God, and she begins to be with others in service, out of a truer healthier sense of identity that does not need to earn love through a false sense of taking care of others. Melissa's service in ministry becomes more Christocentric, more rooted in her own ongoing taste of Mary and Jesus' caring.

At prayer Melissa's imaginative heart experiences diminishing shame as she inwardly dialogues in-the-Spirit while feeling naked and vulnerable at Mary's breast and at Jesus' cross. The very meaning of pain, sorrow, and suffering changes for her. Pain, sorrow, and suffering once caused by deep and subtle self-recriminations, felt unworthiness, and an unhealthy self-protection from relational living now regularly dissipate. Sorrow and suffering are presently experienced primarily as empathetic sharings in Jesus' gentle Heart. She now sees within the lens of sorrow and a suffering-in-love as she becomes more deeply aware of people and social structures that unnecessarily inflict pain on others.

Because Melissa increasingly tastes a mutuality in spousal loving with Jesus and because she feels profoundly "taken care of," there is a sense of divine paradox. A sense of "vacation" is readily felt as accessible in the middle of daily work. She can more freely express angers about her humanity, and there is also a growing desire to share with others. There is even a desire to joyfully share more in Jesus' sufferings to further complete God's kingdom in this world. For Melissa reality has become experienced as being specifically relational. Fundamentally relating with Christ is now her life!

Because of the interpersonal power of sexual images within the context of early childhood issues, a healthy skepticism and caring watchfulness will need to be cultivated in Melissa's new life-in-the-Spirit. Clearly, her fear of being abandoned and her sense of shameful messiness have been touched by God's grace. She feels "washed by Mercy" in nakedness, and this frees her from felt shame. Yet, her desire to "suffer-with-Jesus" requires great attentiveness to future heartfelt movements. Ignatius's Guidelines #328–36, which address the more subtle interior impulses at work in the human heart, should be employed.

Melissa's spiritual insights around the dialectic of "nourishing" consolations enabling her to face "annihilating" desolations can be insidiously turned against her by the evil spirit and/or her own fears. Melissa's heart having been swept clean could experience many demons returning making life more disconsolate (Matt. 12:43–45).

As Melissa experiences deepening care and inner freedom by allowing herself to be with the mediating image of Mary's breast (i.e., Guideline #316) the accompanying consolation strengthens her in God's grace. She becomes capable of facing new depths of interior anguish and pain still affecting her from childhood. The heartfelt movement to stay at the cross within suffering love is a movement inviting her to continue to relate desolations to a God who never abandons her, and who delights in her messy humanity. She can further appropriate eschatological promises which heal her past, carrying her into God's future service for justice. This, however, depends upon Melissa's remaining in a self-emptying interior posture, not assuming control over her insights apart from the affectively mediating images. If Melissa resists a generous deepening receptive participation in the ebb and flow of consolation and desolation she can expect to be shackled by an angel of light through which the evil spirit arouses good feelings so as to focus a person's attention on the wrong things (see Guidelines #331–32).

A creative intensity exists in Melissa's need to accept a new range of accountability for having experienced so great a love. She can easily take on newer and subtler senses of overresponsibility. And this can be done in the name of religious commitment. For example, Melissa could absorb nourishing consolations and begin to try to fix her desolations by masking inner control of mediating images within an effort that speaks of self-improvement rather than self-acceptance.

At one and the same time Melissa needs to say an ongoing "yes" to suffering the world in Love, in Jesus, while refusing to take on pain from within a spiritually unrelated sense of personal responsibility. Melissa's maturation in the Holy Spirit depends upon further reliance on the gratuity of God's faithfulness and Christ's ongoing desire to re-create her. Maturation also depends upon her patiently allowing desolations to "speak," finding God's love present in her own sufferings.

A frequent exercising of gratitude and thankfulness inside Melissa's heart, especially during times of desolation, will greatly protect her from harmful overly responsible efforts. Attempts to fix those human pains which defy fixing only compounds pain. Through participating in Jesus' redeeming, self-emptying embrace of humanity (Phil. 2:3–11) Melissa can grow in holiness.

General Questions for Personal Reflection

1. Does any particular image in your prayer especially elicit felt consolations and/or desolations? Please explain. What happens in your heart when sexual images become present in relational prayer?

2. What is your experience of Mary's presence in faith? Can you go to Mary, the Mother of God, easily and allow her to mediate God's healing graces? Please explain.

Specific Practicum Questions for Spiritual Directors

1. Describe the experience of God's presence amid your sexual energies while working with directees.

2. List the specific "Guidelines for the Discernment of Spirits" (see Appendix I) that you see illuminated in Melissa's story, and name two learnings that you derive from this pastoral diagnostic assessment.

Chapter Four

PAUL'S EXPERIENCE OF HEALING PRAYER

Profile

Paul, age thirty-eight, comes from a middle-class, Eastern European–Irish family background. As a Roman Catholic diocesan priest, he lives celibacy as part of the evangelical call of Jesus' Spirit. Paul was awarded a doctoral degree while studying theology in Europe and maintains a keen interest in the Lutheran-Catholic ecumenical dialogue. Paul serves as a teacher in both a Catholic university and a seminary. His work also includes sacramental ministry in a rural parish on weekends. Travel to China, Italy, and the Middle East broadened Paul's understanding of the slow process of interior conversion to Christ amid cultural diversities. Following his experience of the "retreat house" format for engaging in the Spiritual Exercises, Paul prays "privately/contemplatively" about half an hour a day and "publicly/liturgically" about an hour a day. The Eucharist is received daily.

Summing up his heart's adventure after entering into Ignatius Loyola's Spiritual Exercises Paul states that it was "the most powerful experience of God's love which I have ever encountered."

Interview with Paul

John: "This is Paul, who engaged himself in the Spiritual Exercises within the traditional thirty-day retreat mode. So the first question is,...Take a few seconds in your heart, Paul,...and just ask yourself,... "What was the greatest or one of the greatest experiences of God's love when you look over in your heart...the total experience of the Spiritual Exercises...about a year ago?"

73

Paul: "Well, I think,...without a doubt...the experience of God communicating His love by way of an inner image that...was connected to an outer experience and became kind of God's vehicle for loving me....

"What happened in prayer was...the experience of praying with the Gospel of the Annunciation,...and...experiencing an invitation to hold the Christ Child, which...immediately took me back to an experience of only a month earlier of...holding or being held...almost by a child,...a real physical child, at some friend's home in Italy, in Rome. The experience of that was kind of a surprise and an experience of...kind of a gentle trust that a child would have to put himself in...to want to be held...even by a stranger. And for me that experience came back in prayer and was a way into...both experiencing God's love for me and my love for God. The felt experience of...experience with a real child...became a way of imagining myself being held by God. In a way, it was definitely an experience of grace. It was not at all a thought-out process. It was very spontaneous...and I never in a million years would have connected the two experiences."

John: "I encourage you to just be with what was or is grace...in that spirit of repetition in the Exercises,...with the belief that letting yourself reexperience some of this...and repeating some of this... will actually have its own meaning for now. That being said,...could you say a little bit more about what the experience was like with the image that brought back that experience from being with the child in Italy. If you could just say...focus on...what that felt like...and describe what happened in the experience."

Paul: "Well, in being invited, in prayer,...to hold the Christ Child, ...in allowing myself to do that,...I guess first of all,...it was a felt experience. I mean,...it was as though I was holding that child back in Italy,...which for me was an experience of surprise...for starters. The...I had been sitting talking with the child's father and really very unaware of the child's presence...and all of a sudden he kind of crawled up on me...and he was sort of resting very comfortably. And...it was surprising...even for the father. He said, 'Well, he doesn't usually do that....He's very shy with strangers.' And so on. So it was an odd experience in itself,...a very beautiful experience of warmth and of a child's love,...and of the child's contentment to be there. And so...when all of that came back...in the experience of prayer,... it was an experience for me of... imaging myself being held by God! Somehow... there was a naturalness to it,... That I belonged there. And also, I guess,... remembering my own feelings ... however spontaneous and unthought out... of love for that real child, imagining, you know,... God's love for me in that position, in that situation. And yet, you know,... not just equating the two feelings, but also knowing that God's love must be so much more. And being very filled with, you know,... that thought... and, you know, how much...I don't know if I would have said it that way at the time,... but how much more. If it's God,... how much more love there must be... for me."

John: "And can you say... with that thought... and in that experience... could you just name the heartfelt feelings that emerged in that experience?"

Paul: "Well,...I guess I'll start with what would be obvious. I mean, it sounds obvious,... but in the experience maybe not,... an overwhelming experience of God's love for me and,...I guess,... emphasizing 'for me' and emphasizing 'felt.' I had come on retreat ... really seeking an experience of God's love *for me*. And,... like everybody else in the world... having a cerebral, intellectual understanding that is probably... must be true... if God is God... and I am who I am.... But it was never on the level of *felt* experience. And in that experience of prayer, it was on the level of a felt experience. It was God. It was me. It was a feeling of... naturalness and ... also a certain sense of awe... and tremendous... being the object of God's love was... a tremendous feeling of... well, of being loved! ... An experience of freedom,... Of not having to do anything to be loved by God, but simply like a child who is not conscious... of... that kind of game playing, I guess, that... maybe older people are... that it was right that I belonged there,... that it was right that God loved me. And I didn't... it wasn't something that...I had to in any way prove or earn."

John: "And... it's okay to answer yes or no to this next question,... But has that experience of God's love stayed with you?... That experience *for me*,... the felt awe and freedom... has that stayed with you? And secondly,... does that experience affect how you think or feel or act, now,... in the present?"

Paul: "I guess I'd answer a yes and a no. I'll take the no first. Obviously, ... the experience of the retreat being very, very powerful and overwhelming, ... there's a sense in which that sometimes fades ... and I don't have, ... at every single moment, ... a sense of closeness to God. In the ups and downs of life, ... that fades. On the other hand ... the experience was so, ... I guess I'll us the word 'foundational,' ... that many times I find it a way into prayer. For instance, ... it's not uncommon that in praying privately, ... praying on a daily basis, ... I would actually even physically position my hands in such a way ... that I can imagine holding a child.... And that physical sensation ... allows me instantly to be in touch with the experience of being held by God. And ... that continues with a pretty fair degree of regularity. And coupled with that, ... even at times when I, ... let's say for whatever reason, ... I may not be explicitly feeling that kind of experience ... that deep love of God, ... Even at those times ... the experience of retreat is so clear to me ... that ... I can never deny that it happened. It's not like ... a neat idea ... that sort of existed for awhile ... and sort of has gotten relegated to the realm of memory, ... kind of a pleasant memory ... that can be conjured up. But ... it's such a positive experience, ... that even if at the moment ... when for whatever reason I may not be knowing why I'm not experiencing God's love in such a strong way, ... I know that I have ... and that's a tremendous sense of consolation for me. It's like an undeniable fact of my life. And so in that sense, ... it's always with me. It's as real to me as ... the fact that we are having a conversation right now. It's very natural ... you know, ... that the experience was true and is true."

John: "The naturalness ... you have used that word ... not to analyze it ... but I just noticed that you have used that word a couple of times ... the naturalness of the experience in the retreat and now, ... even amid the ups and downs, ... How do you feel ... naturally now, ... recalling living in that fact ... in the immediate moment or ... an example from recent days? The question ... let me put it succinctly. The naturalness of being with God in that love ... as a child ... and entering into prayer the way you said it happens ... almost instantly? I guess, all I'm asking is, ... in the present ... what do you feel inside ... walking with that naturally? What do you feel inside as you talk about it, walk with it, ... that experience of God's love of you as a child?"

Paul: "If I understand the question,...I think, I used the word before...'foundational'...and that sounds kind of heavy duty...and almost abstract,...but it's like having a rock-bottom...foundation to my life...that even in the midst of other kinds of struggles and other,...you know,...moments where, yeah,...I may not be ecstatically feeling consoled or the presence of God,...the memory...and I used the word before,...a *bodily* memory,...that it's much more than the cerebral idea of memory...that in itself is...very consoling...in that a present struggle...is easier to take...or it's...that's certainly the unnatural experience of life. The natural, the real,...the true experience,...is the experience of resting in God's love. That's kind of the norm. I mean, it's not the exception anymore. And anything that kind of...deviates from that norm...is the exception. I don't know if that makes any sense. But...it's just much more of a ...reality, I guess. I don't know quite what else to say. I don't know if you want to ask it again?"

John: "That's fine. You've answered it...several times. What was the greatest experience of struggle...as you recall the Exercises?...The greatest experience of inner struggle...with relating to God,...with Jesus' Spirit?"

Paul: "Well, I guess a couple of things come to my mind. I think they are ultimately related,...but for me though...the beginning of retreat...had it's own set of difficulties....Not that I wasn't happy to be doing what I was doing, or that I had a sense that I was not supposed to be doing it....Yeah, it was the flat land and the no trees and the no mountains that drove me crazy....But, anyway, ...the initial struggle was,...I don't know how else to put it,... but trying to figure out *how*...what I had done in three years of psychotherapy...was somehow related to this. I knew that it was ...in some way...and yet,...I didn't know how to let it be,...I guess. So,...fairly early on in the retreat...I think I...some of my attempts at prayer were kind of,...'I'm going to win this one for Jesus,'...in the sense of, you know,...I'll get this prayer figured out ...sort of...one way or the other. And with a tremendous sense of emptiness...as a result...sort of and confusion and...almost a listless sort of...experience. But...I remember, we had a conversation ...one of those days...and you had encouraged me very much to... allow myself to experience...inner images and things that had been part of the psychotherapy route....And to just sort of sit with that

...and I don't know whether it was by explicit suggestion or by implication...to acknowledge that that was in some sense...already
in the presence of God.... Or God was present to *it*. I think that's
kind of the best way to phrase it. And...that was...well, it was the
experience...I mean, that it was so true that just being present...
allowing myself, including my inner world,...very gently and without pressure and without a lot of...thought...or anxiety...to be
present to God,...that it immediately then opened up...the way to
prayer. I mean...God was clearly part of all that...and I began experiencing the presence of God...in the midst of those images. Also
what comes to my mind in talking about struggle...and in some way
...probably is related,...when things in the retreat,...however,...
moved into trying to pray about,...trying to understand sin. What
is sin? What is it's meaning? That, too,...seemed to throw me into
an awful lot of struggle...and...maybe a kind of similar experience of the struggles...at the beginning of the retreat?...Kind of a
real,...I'm going to take this by storm approach,...but with no suc-
cess, with no...(quite the contrary)...an experience of...upset and
...self-doubt and recrimination,...what am I doing wrong?...that
this is not working. And...again,...a very specific memory of a...
suggestion (on your part)...you had given me (probably to reread),
...maybe I had read it once already. I don't remember exactly who
the author was,...but trying to comment on the meaning of sin and
what that is. That one way of looking at sin...is untruth,...accep-
tance of falsehood,...living by way of falsehood. And...as soon as
I read that, it immediately clicked...and became again a kind of an
opening into...a much deeper prayer. In some way,...I think for
me,...sinfulness...has to do with false ideas about myself...who
I am,...not allowing myself to rest in the truth of who God is revealing me to be. And, it's sort of a key...metaphor,...a key word
for understanding sinfulness. Not that I...I think I'm still struggling
with that...I'm trying to...come to grips with what sinfulness is
and how it works. But...clearly,...that was sort of a way out of
those struggles...and definitely says something to me...about what
sinfulness is."

John: "Well, you know,...over and over in the retreat there was this
...sometimes is was explicit...sometimes it wasn't,...this application of senses,...where the disengagement from overintellectualizing
or analyzing,...being cerebral, as you said...we both saw God con-

stantly inviting...into something Ignatius calls the application of senses,...just letting oneself notice and feel with all five senses,... the grandeur of God,...the beauty of God all around us...and as I say that...I remember part of the retreat, so I'm smiling. I had forgotten,...you forget these things...until you start to talk....So, the question that I'd like to simply ask now is,...Remembering the application of senses...or remembering the noncerebral invitations to prayer,...is there anything else that stands out as...an experience of God's love? The primary experience was the resting in God as a child. Could you describe any other experience that stands out as a highlight of...being with God's love, being in God's love?"

Paul: "Particularly in terms of applications of senses....Well, a couple things come to mind. Probably I could get on a roll I would imagine, so you can stop me. A lot of them. This is in no particular order...or indication of depth, but...one thing that pops into my mind is the experience of music on retreat. A lot of people, you know,...I'm a musician and, you know,...and people imagine that I'm always living in music, which...I don't think I am. But on retreat...with *great* frequency...and I would say maybe three quarters of retreat, or at least half,...very often in the experience of prayer...I would hear specific pieces of music. And pieces, generally speaking,...musicians would call romantic,...romantic in the sense of Chopin, opera, other things that...very kind of free, joyful,...very passionate kind of music. But I would hear it in great detail...that I can almost...(it would be a specific recording)...or I could imagine myself...playing it...certain pieces of music that I had studied several years ago...came back to me in not only listening to them, but...you know, part of my own process of...the way a piece of music is memorized...is not so much that I see notes and then play it,...but it's a feeling...a feeling of my hands on a keyboard. And that's really how music is memorized,...at least as far as I'm concerned. So,...certain pieces that I hadn't thought about in years returned...and I could have written them out...note for note, ...just because I had felt them...in the experience of prayer. And, of course, the strange thing is...that normally I would have imagined that as being like a distraction. Okay, let's put the music aside ...so we can really get on with prayer....But the fun thing was that ...I allowed myself to experience that as part of God's love. Very often,...again over a substantial period of time,...that the music coincided with my own strong feelings...that I was experiencing in terms of Susan. The experience of...physically being with her, allowing myself to feel love for her,...feeling free enough to admit that that was really true, that that was really going on. And feeling...okay about that...gradually,...ever so slowly...being able to say yes to that,...to enjoy that...and to really believe...that God was the author of that...and not myself. I mean, a lot of these experiences were just too spontaneous, and at the same time in too much detail, and too much specificity...to be kind of conjured up by myself."

John: "Just a pause before you go on to other experiences. In that specificity,...what did you feel in your heart?"

Paul: "Well, an overwhelming feeling of God's love. I mean, it's just ...again, an experience...that I just knew...that it was *not* me, ...that it was God loving me more and more. After awhile,...I can remember laughing one day after one of our conversations,... I don't know whether I expressed it. But, oh, I know! Yes, I *do* know! Probably within the last week of retreat...what came to my mind was an experience of a particular piece of music from the Neo-Catechumenate group...and it was a Hebrew song that they would sing...and the Hebrew word was *dayenue;* but the piece was...'It Would Have Been Enough.' And the song was,...it would have been enough that Abraham came....But then you gave us Moses....It would have been enough that you gave us Moses....But then you also gave us the promised land. And everything...one thing after another...a big litany...of God's wonderful experiences...experiences of God's love,...one thing better than the next. And by that time in the retreat,...I was kind of laughing...like, okay, what's next? You know,...allowing myself to believe...that God really wanted to love me more and more,...And very concrete evidence of that on retreat....Experience after experience. So it was kind of always...being surprised...and *overwhelmed* by God's love...time after time.

"Another experience,...strange...and kind of mixed...initially not knowing...what it was all about. In coming to say, 'yes'...to my own experience of God's love and allowing myself to feel love, ...allowing myself to feel love for Susan...and to really...well, we talked so much about desire...and what does it mean? What are my deepest desires? And where is God in all that? But also dealing with something mysterious called 'the *death* of desire,'...and trying to understand what that's all about. Allowing myself to both feel desire and to give those desires to God...in prayer,...was for me a tremendous experience...(I don't know how else to express it)... other than the experience of death. And a...a tremendous amount of struggle surrounding that. But I guess what I'm thinking of is ...the upshot of that was...experiencing the *removal* of the fear of death...of my own physical death,...which is something that I was certainly much more fearful of. After the experience of trying to give to God my own desires...and experiencing that as a death,... I have...in prayer...a very powerful experience of...it was being taken back to...the experience of...Pope Paul VI's funeral (which I had attended)...and a number of memories of that. But *particularly* the experience of the conclusion of the funeral...as his casket was being carried into St. Peter's Basilica for burial...and...there was a commentary over a loud speaker system that had accompanied that...And that very simply said something to the effect...that the body of the Holy Father is carried into the basilica were it will rest in the ground awaiting its resurrection to glory. And...it's a very powerful memory,...but in rekindling the memory, I guess, it was ...the sense of the *tremendous strength* of God's life, the power of the resurrection....God's loving us through death and,...you know, the promise of life...that is so strong that one can face death,... I'm sure with a certain amount of human fear,...but with a lot of that removed because of (in my case)...the experience of God's love. And the experience of...in some way, in some strange way, ...that I don't really understand,...already tasting death...now... and surviving that,...And knowing that...somehow, I could survive physical death, too.

"What comes back to me at the same time...was...a line that I have read in a book by Thomas Merton,...that I was reading on retreat....These aren't his words,...but words of someone he was studying about and writing about. And,...let's see if I can remember the words: 'What magnificent form will blaze in things perpetual, when even now, it is so lovely in things perishing.' That to see a blaze of God's glory in nature,...in human life and in that experience of Paul VI's funeral,...to see...in some sense God's glory and beauty ...how much *more* beautiful, how much *more* blazing is certainly what lies ahead. So all of those things together...made for a very powerful experience of God's love...and on and on and on."

John: "Can you say,... as always I'll push you to the limit,... and if we're at the limit, that's fine,... but can you say anything further, ... sort of drawing back inside... and letting yourself taste, retaste that struggle with death and the blazing glory of resurrection,... of freedom,... from some of the fear.... Can you say anything more about what the struggle felt like... and what the freedom felt like, ... feels like?"

Paul: "The death of desire? That's what I thought you meant,... but I just thought I'd check it, just in case I was in error. This may be cruel and inhuman punishment, but I can deal with it!

"Okay, well,... one of the patterns on retreat that came through again and again... and certainly came through very powerfully in this experience is that,... for some strange reason... I would get myself into a position, and I think this is probably... it is a life pattern, ... being presented with two... impossible options... that at some time of decision or conflict,... it just seems like it's A or B. And neither A or B are a workable solution. There's just something wrong with both solutions... so that it seems unsolvable... or, um... can't be figured out... or just, you know,... nothing to do. In this case, ... having spent two or so glorious weeks coming to terms with my own experience of desire, my own experience of love, my own experience of love for Susan in particular,... and appreciating the beauty of that,... trying to reconcile that with being an ordained priest for twelve years... and loving that... and knowing that that is a part of me and so on. I seem to be in the situation of being between two unreconcilable situations. On the one hand,... it didn't seem like I was going to leave the priesthood... or should or wanted to. On the other hand... a great affirming that... I would allow my experience of Susan to be relegated to the realm of the unreal... and that that would be just totally denied... and I didn't want to do that either, because that seemed to be a foolish thing to do. So... two things that seemed impossible to hold together... until this death of desire thing came by,... the idea that... I mean... I was invited to consider the idea that somehow... God could... and was inviting me to actually hold those two things together,... that giving that desire to God, ... which is a death,... God would somehow... not allow that desire to disappear,... that if it really was part of me, if it really is part of me,... then it has to remain part of me. But that somehow... in giving it to God, God would work that out. Now, that sounded pretty unreal. And...I certainly didn't jump at the opportunity to embrace that. And yet, over a period of time it became pretty clear...that that was probably what I was being invited to do. And somehow, I mean, I can remember...the moment, I guess you'd say,...praying about that,...being somewhat confused...and maybe half believing. I can remember very directly talking to God and saying, 'Okay, only because I believe that this is you,...that somehow you are behind this,...I will offer to you my own desires, my own love for Susan,...my own wonderful experience of love...and I hope you're there to kind of catch this. And for me,...I was almost...like jumping off a cliff, I guess. And I don't know...that at the moment, you know,...we all long for trumpet blasts and flashes of lightning,...I don't know that that was experienced. Somehow I was able to say, 'Yes, Lord,...here, take this' The only reason why I'm saying this is because somehow I think it's you...that's really doing this,...Otherwise it just makes absolutely no sense at all. And it wasn't until... later,...maybe the next day,...and I don't remember when,...that it became clear to me that the fruit of that was,...at least one fruit of it was,...the removing of the fear of physical death. And I began to understand that what had happened was that there had been some tasting of death...in that experience. I had other experiences that kind of confirmed that. It just...I remember later in prayer too, having...somehow in a quiet and gentle way,...I knew that it was a participation in the death of Jesus *Himself!* That it was a taste of that...in some strange way. I don't know how. But...the death of Jesus,...redemptive for the world,...a giving of one's life...that somehow I had entered into that in some way,...I had tasted that. Again,...not knowing fully how or even what that means today. But ...it was somewhat like being in the heart of Christ...and feeling... what that kind of giving means,...that kind of death,...which is a giving.

"That experience...It was a very gentle experience...I mean, very clear. I know that's really what it was. Again, not with trumpet blasts and flashes of lightning, but...that I had been loved by God...even in that,...in being allowed to taste,...in some beautiful way,...the experience of Jesus' own dying. Somehow connected to that...was an experience in prayer,...that in a sense if you will, ...had been *brewing* throughout retreat,...the experience of kissing the Heart of Christ...as a sign of my own love. And that too,...initially, I mean...there was a lot of resistance to that. But...without

a lot of fireworks, ... but a very natural and sort of beautiful invitation. And ... it was somehow like being in the Heart of God, I guess,
... to have some knowledge of God's love, I guess, ... for the world,
... for me. Like not in some odd, ... like I've got something nobody
else has got ... kind of experience, ... but almost very natural, ... that
this was a natural result of what had happened in prayer ... in the
death of desire."

John: "We are going to go into the litany of before-and-after reflections. Remember when we do this litany from the worksheet called
'The Inner Heart of My Faith,' ... that it's more than okay to leave
segments blank or unanswered. You know, ... not everybody answers
all of the categories. Some people do. So ... whatever is true to your
own experience ... What would you say, Paul, ... was your philosophy of life before making the Spiritual Exercises ... and what is it
now in the present? And I ask you to keep your answers brief ... at
this point."

Paul: "Okay, brief, ... that's a tough question. I think the philosophy
of life, ... somewhat slugging it out for Jesus, ... I guess, before. And
in the sense that I'm a dutiful person and, ... not without ... that I
was without a real faith or something like that, ... but never experiencing what I experienced on retreat, ... a powerful experience of
God's love. It was much more, always an experience, ... more of a
one-sided experience. I mean, ... I knew God loved me ... and all of
that kind of stuff, ... but I'll do my duty for God. After retreat, ...
naturally a certain amount of that is still with me, that's who I am.
But much more ... it's allowing God to love me, you know, ... the
philosophy is ... trying to just, to accept what God wants to do ...
for me, ... trying to overcome resistance to that. Today one of my
favorite lines in the Psalms comes, ... 'Surrender to God and He will
do everything for you.' Not that I experience that every day, but ...
I guess that's more of it, you know, ... seeking. I find myself these
days praying more and more for faith, ... not in the sense of, you
know, ... make me strong to go out there and win the world, ... but
just simply the faith to accept that day by day, moment by moment,
God is leading, ... God is loving. And the more I surrender to that
... the more things are right, the more ... I mean, ... I just know that
that's the way to live. It doesn't happen all the time, but I mean, I'm
praying for that a lot."

John: "And what was your greatest fear or anxiety before making the Spiritual Exercises... and what would you say that is now... in your experience?"

Paul: "My greatest fear... not about the Exercises, but just,... I guess... death,... that sounds odd but I have plenty of fears... and I still do... but in terms of big time... I feel very embarrassed... even saying that. And I don't know if I would have owned up to it even... before it became clear during the retreat... that this was something God was working out. But I think that's true."

John: "What would you say is your greatest fear now?"

Paul: "Losing the experience of retreat. That's... there's a side of me that says, you know,... no... I mean that's a very powerful experience. On the other hand,... it was so good and the experience of retreat was good and,... you know, in so many ways... formative and foundational. The idea that somehow... I could be *radically* off the track... and somehow lose that orientation. I think I fear that."

John: "Okay,... continuing with the litany,... What would be your greatest experience of joy or gratitude... before you made the Spiritual Exercises... and now,... in the present?"

Paul: "Before retreat,... I guess maybe... scattered things. In some sense, I guess,... the joy of being a priest... and doing the things a priest does. Maybe certain specific joys associated with that,... a good experience of helping somebody... and being a positive influence on somebody,... all of which, I mean,... even as I say that,... I'm very aware of that being more of a task-oriented side. And I think there's a certain truth to that. Postretreat,... I think that my experiences of joy are relational.... Certainly, with Susan. I have a great time when I'm with her. I have allowed myself to have much more fun than I ever did. Joy, in... continuing experiences of relating to God. Not all of the time, every day, but... relishing some of that. ... Enjoying music with God.... But even then,... I mean, it's a very different experience. Allowing myself to pray with music. I mean,... like, nontraditional religious music, opera, for instance."

John: "What was... this can be a tough one... what was your greatest experience of sorrow before making the Spiritual Exercises?"

Paul: "I'm going to make a quick look to the sheet here. Yeah,... I had put down loneliness. I think, yeah,... that's very true,... loneliness in a pervasive sort of sense. I mean,... almost,... which when I look at it... is certainly a good portion of the reason why I sought out psychotherapy, I think. I also put down Joe Stauffer's death. Joe, who had been a pastor and a friend here,... I would say a real experience of sorrow,... but in a... in a deeper or... a good sense. I don't know,... maybe that sounds odd? Sorrow,... as one would at the death of a good friend,... but in terms of more pervasive,... definitely the experience of loneliness."

John: "And now after the Exercises,... what is your greatest experience of sorrow?"

Paul: "I think it's struggle times,... times where... maybe I'm not as in touch with a felt experience of God's love... as I would like to be. And I don't know what to do with that... or can't seem to work my way through... whatever is not allowing that to happen."

John: "Is the loneliness still there?"

Paul: "No,... I don't think so,... not,... I think it's in the realm of the normal,... I mean, there are certain times, but no,... I have to say that that's qualitatively different. I just don't,... on a human level,... on a level with God... I don't think I sense that,... I mean, it's hard to imagine,... even looking back on it,... to what degree... preretreat loneliness... affected my life. I look sometimes at... let's say even my... in the last year... maybe even somewhat prior to retreat,... but certainly much, much more after retreat,... my own amount of time spent with and time enjoyed with Susan. It's like night and day! I mean,... I can't believe sometimes that I'm living the same life. And I'm certainly... you know,... I'm doing every bit as much, or I'm externally kind of living the same way,... but *qualitatively* it's like night and day."

John: "The next question in the litany... is also very deep,... is a very all-encompassing question.... You spoke a lot about desire in your stories.... This question is,... What was your greatest heartfelt desire before the retreat?"

Paul: "As spontaneously as I formulated this, or became aware of this desire,... I think it's very true. I think it was... to know the love of God for me... personally. It came out as I was preparing for retreat, and someone asked me the question,... Why are you going on retreat? And, that's what I answered. And I really think that that's, ... it wasn't just a momentary thought. It was a longstanding desire."

John: "And what's your greatest heartfelt desire now,... qualitatively? Would you verbalize it in a different way... or is it the same ... or...?"

Paul: "Well, it's certainly not the same in the sense that,... the experience of retreat... very much brought the experience of God's love, ... but there's a desire for *more*. There's a desire to be in that. I mean, having tasted it,... to return to it,... To more fully,... on a more longstanding basis, you know,... greater depth, to experience that love."

John: "Any specificity in the greatest heartfelt desire... to experience more of God's love?"

Paul: "I guess... I'd like to give myself permission to taste... a little bit more of God loving me through my own desire,... and my own love for Susan,... to be freer to say yes to that, which I'm struggling with. That has become an issue.

John: "Two more questions.... Paul,... how would you say you regarded yourself... before making the Spiritual Exercises... and is there a qualitative difference as to how you regard yourself now?"

Paul: "I think you've added a question to the litany. I don't remember that one. How I regarded myself before?... Although I would have been hard-pressed to identify it,... I think... a certain side of me,... I felt very much like a child,... an immaturity in a person who's, you know,... thirty-eight... and doing fairly responsible things in life,... and also an adolescent... in a certain sense, you know,... there are clearly two figures... two inner images that I've been dealing with in psychotherapy. But they are very real... and very real portions of myself... without making it into some big deal beforehand. And after,... those images are still part of me, but... there's no doubt... that the child image... having been a focal point of the retreat and of God's loving me... has somewhat been healed. And I think,... I think still certainly that God wants to love me as a child,... but it doesn't have the pain of immaturity or a childishness. Sometimes it does,... I think, some of that's still there. I think the adolescent image,... I think, is still being worked on. That's a more vibrant image in the sense that I think still,... in my inner world,...

needs to be paid attention to. I think...in some way...God is still doing something with that. But again,...I think it's less painfully so,...less isolated. So, I think, it's *in God*...and so for that reason is less,...you know, this unfortunate part of myself...that kind of hangs there."

John: "And the last question is simply...What was your image of God...and your experience of God's regard before the retreat (in some ways you've answered this)...but just to hone in on it in a pointed way,...What was your image of God...before the retreat and your experience of God's regard for you...and what's that like now?"

Paul: "I think my image of God or...God's way of looking at me,... prior to the retreat, you know,...a benign in some sense,...powerful person,...but rather distant. Intellectually, I mean, knowing that there was some overwhelming love there...somewhere. And yet,... on a felt level, always kind of juggling with,...well, when people are distant, we're never quite sure what their intentions are as much as we think they're benign,...we're never quite sure. So postretreat, ...the experience of being loved by God,...as a Father would love a son,...kind of warmth, of intimacy, of presence, of faithfulness, ...you know, sometimes not necessarily colored in,...like not a vivid visual image...as much as a *felt sense* of my being held,... being held by God. And that was a strong part of retreat, and that continues."

John: "And...just as a brief summary statement,...how would you describe what happened to you in making the Spiritual Exercises... and how has that affected how you live today?"

Paul: "Small question!...Succinctly put,...for me...it was on one hand, an experience of...integrating what I had done in psychotherapy with God, which was no small thing. I mean, it was a definite experience of being loved by God in that experience,...in a way that ...*far* surpassed anything that I could have ever imagined....Never would have dreamed that it would have been so integrated. And also ...opening up to,...by grace, being able to accept God's love for me. I mean, in funny, crazy ways,...in relationships, in music,...in the world around me. I mean, intellectually,...I knew that that was all right or good or possible,...but it was impossible,...actually. And to be able to,...in some sense receive that from God,...not perfectly or all the time, ... but ... just to know that God is present in ... my own feelings of excitement about a piece of music ... or a person. That's definitely part of retreat. And live differently? ... Well, yeah, ... I mean, I said before ... I'm just *relating* differently ... to Susan very concretely, ... but I mean, it's like night and day! And if I stop and think about it, ... it's hard to believe it's the same life. In enjoying another person, ... enjoying Susan particularly, ... and in believing that she enjoys my being with her ... (as much as I enjoy my being with her), ... and allowing myself to believe that, to relish that, ... to make that an important part of my life ... (without feeling awful about that ... or strange). ... But now I believe that God is present in that."

John: "I'll add an important question. In relating to other people and other things, ... is that also qualitatively different? ... Just to recap."

Paul: "Yeah, ... the experience, let's say, ... of God in the beauty of the world around me. I mean, ... I have not turned into a Franciscan, ... but I mean ... to really allow myself to relish ... the enjoyment of a beautiful day, ... to be surprised about, let's say, ... my relationships with students, ... to be more confident that God is leading me and to have confidence that I am living in God. God is personally, actively present. I am relating to everything differently. ... For instance ... I'm participating in an adult faith-sharing group now. That's somewhat miraculous. That wasn't me before. I never would have permitted myself to relate like that, ... to enjoy like that. And ... spiritual direction has picked up too. More people are asking me for spiritual direction ... and I'm enjoying that more."

Summary

Paul expressed a desire to enter into the mystical dynamic of the Spiritual Exercises out of the deeper desire to receive and taste God's love more personally. Paul's interior ripeness and ability to readily exercise his spirit in conversation with Jesus' Spirit was promoted by several years of psychotherapy, and especially an ordinary willingness to generously follow nourishing desires that brought him enjoyment, serving others as a priest and musician.

The exterior Word of God in the Annunciation story evoked a natural awe-inspiring interior image of Paul's holding the Christ child.

The interpenetrating grace of praying with the Ignatian application
of senses led Paul's heart to remember a recent actual experience of
having received surprising enjoyment while holding a close friend's
baby son. Further surprise was tasted as Paul permitted himself in
prayer to rest in and follow his deepest felt consolations. An imaginative juxtaposition then occurred within Paul's heart, seeing and
feeling himself being held by God, as the very object of God's loving
delight.

Extraordinary personal love from God was bestowed and felt.
Though the magnitude of the consolation received can be partially
explained because of Paul's developmental ripeness and because of
powerful mediating images, the lasting quality of sensible healing
grace illuminates a radiant instance of what Ignatius Loyola calls
"consolation without previous cause." In other words, the qualitative depth of Paul's affective experience of consolation is not possible
to explain except by pointing to the sole desire and initiatives of
Jesus' creating Spirit. Paul's heart received a quality of healing grace
that dramatically alters how he feels, thinks, and relates to himself,
music, nature, and God's presence. Love's searing truth taught Paul
who he is, an image of Christ, a son of God. Love's burning desire in Jesus' Spirit gave him (in-spired) an in-depth heart knowing,
a "body memory" about how unconditionally loved he is resting in
God's arms. So strong was this consolation that Paul experiences an
inability to deny the abiding reality of God's personal loving many
months later amid the ups and downs of life. He returns prayerfully
to this "body memory" and accesses healing grace by repetitiously
reentering this consolation through practicing Ignatius's application
of the senses. Paul daily repeats permitting himself to refrain from
overanalyzing mystery, simply *being with* the interior leadings of the
most strongly felt consolations.

From this "foundational" experience of "tremendous consolation" flows numerous healing graces. Pervasive loneliness carried
from childhood becomes permanently altered by spiritual relational
loving. Paul finds himself immensely enjoying the experience of
falling in love with Susan and desires to stay in love with her. Simultaneously, a conflicting desire to remain a celibate priest wells up,
a wanting to continue to enjoy that ministerial identity. An incredible healing unfolds, freeing Paul from the fear of physical death, as
he prays within these conflicting interior consolations. In the middle
of an overriding desire to single-mindedly taste more and more of

God's personal love, Paul receives a felt invitation to take a radical leap in relational trust, giving himself to God alone, placing all his desires in Jesus' Heart. Initially, reluctance and bafflement surfaced inside of Paul's heart, though he ends up generously entrusting all his desires to Christ. What transpires again overtakes Paul with awe and surprise. Spontaneously moved to pray from within the remembered details of Pope Paul VI's funeral, the great strength and power of Jesus as Love resurrecting gloriously is experienced through an actual participation in Jesus' death. Paul then inwardly tastes new inner freedom to be a priest, celibately in love with Susan. The conflicting consolations and desires become merged in a felt unity of personal loving in Jesus' Heart.

So long as Paul stays faithful to resting in mystery, he grows in spiritual freedom and feels increasingly loved. Whenever he tries to figure out the personal mystery, in an overly cerebral, distant relating with God, Paul experiences inner resistance and feels desolate. Relationships have been made new for Paul. He enjoys life more so as he participates in and receives nourishment from an adult faith sharing group. Each day carries a great new confidence because Paul knows that he is being held lovingly by God.

A hermeneutic of discerning caution needs to accompany Paul's new sets of spiritual relationships. Their meaning can become skewed and Paul may be duped by the evil spirit, if he does not exercise surrendering all of his desires, regularly returning them as gifts, back to Christ the giver of these interpersonal gifts. In Guideline #322 Ignatius cautions, reminding that felt desolations will come when and if a person begins to love just God's gifts rather than God. Any gift can become an idol through which the invitation to taste Christ's joy is minimized or replaced by a pursuit of lesser pleasures derived from God's good gifts. Also, in Guideline #334 Ignatius cautions, urging retreatants to recognize how they have occasionally been set up to be duped by inner tendencies bending toward minimizing the livelihood of Christ's Spirit.

Paul's desolations usually emanate from a primary wound of felt isolation carrying with it intense loneliness. He possesses a tendency to remain stuck within this root desolation through slipping into "intellectual overdrive" symptomatic of unacknowledged and/or unrelated fears and pride.

Now that Paul's felt isolation has been broken wide open through his attention to the interplay of Christ's indwelling Spirit living amid his inner desiring, the new sets of relationships (especially the gift of Susan) could become ends in themselves. It is important to notice that Paul's conflictual consolations from desiring to enjoy more loving from Susan as well as to exercise ministerial celibate priesthood are initially resolved through a surrender of both desires, both gifts, in relating to the Heart that has provided these beautiful gifts, Christ's Heart.

In following the Lord of the dance, Paul and his spiritual director must remain open to allowing the interior impulses of the Holy Spirit to have sway. And where will this dance of conflicting consoling desires lead in Paul's life, if he courageously relates them again and again to Christ? A new understanding of celibate loving has emerged, inclusive of experiencing erotic love for Susan. Yet many personal dimensions of relating with Susan and with celibate ministerial identity are unexplored. This set of fundamental relationships is new in Paul's personal life in the Holy Spirit. The mystery of the interplay of desires requires him to single-mindedly seek first God's kingdom (Luke 12:29–31). Then Paul will be free enough from unrelated fears, free enough to continually increase his participating in the Trinitarian dance with the Holy Spirit.

Questions will naturally arise around Paul's desires to continue to grow in more love with Susan while wanting to enjoy more ministerial joy as a celibate priest. Is his celibacy flowing from a true charism where interior loneliness is met by God's grace, gifting the church with a prophetic sign of God's reign? Or is Paul's celibacy based upon in-depth fears which have not yet surfaced and which have prevented him from relating to God through loving and marrying a woman? Is his love for Susan a healthy infatuation? Will Paul allow this gift of Susan's friendship to carry him beyond itself into a deepening life with Christ, a life beyond the gift itself?

Interpersonal real answers will emerge whenever Paul generously attends to the mystery of the revelatory power and healing grace calling deep within his experiences of desolation. Their valuable messages will announce the Lord's will and way, the promised advent of more consolation, more spiritual freedom in the Holy Spirit's eternal round dance (John 14:18–20).

General Questions for Personal Reflection

1. Attending to your senses of seeing, hearing, tasting, smelling, and touching, where and how are you most naturally able to receive an affective imaginative sense of being lovingly held by God? Please describe this manner of experiencing grace.

2. Are you able and willing to meditate on the death of a close friend and/or your own impending physical death? What happens between yourself and Jesus' Spirit when you dare to enter into this context for praying?

Specific Practicum Questions for Spiritual Directors

1. Name the most strongly felt inner desires that well up during your serving others as a spiritual director. Now describe living-in-Jesus' Spirit amid the self-emptying, letting-go experience known as the "death of desires."

2. Role play teaching Paul the Ignatian "Guidelines for the Discernment of Spirits" (Appendix I) by pointing to illustrations in his own story.

Chapter Five

LEARNINGS AND
IMPLICATIONS

The life process of everyday mysticism educates the believer's heart through ongoing experiences of healing grace. The Spiritual Exercises, insofar as they bring persons in touch with Christ's living Spirit, represent an educational anthropology carrying a form of scriptural authority. Because Ignatian mysticism roots itself in heart-knowing, it instructs the whole person amid the interpersonal dynamism of interior conversation with biblical portraits of Jesus. Retreatants encountering themselves in relationship with Christ through the Spiritual Exercises come to understand that "the heart must learn so to speak, what it is to be."[1] They come to taste, see, and treasure the harmonizing influence of the Holy Spirit's activity revealing God's reign (Luke 12:32–34). Profound perceptual changes occur within retreatants' hearts as inner affections, the lens through which we see and relate, become shaped by Christ's Spirit's personal loving (1 John 4:13–17).

In studying religious affections at work in prayer Don Saliers writes:

> The concept of the heart, then, is strangely authoritative in Scripture because it gathers to a focal point a whole range of ordinary ways in which human beings explain themselves to each other. We understand ourselves as members of the human race and make ourselves clear to one another by describing our fears, hopes, loves, joys, — in short, our intentions and motives. The human race being what it is, there are no general psychological or sociological laws and behavioral theories which comprehend the richness and authority of these more ordinary ways of describing and explaining our lives. So "the heart" not only explains what we do, it governs who we are.[2]

By continuing to listen for, acknowledge, and respond to Jesus' Spirit speaking effectively through their heartfelt movements, each of the retreatants come to "learn to tell God's story as their story. They each become able to explain how they analogously were oppressed in Egypt and how God liberates, guides and heals them."[3]

From these four narrative portraits we can see illuminated the anthropological foundation of the Spiritual Exercises. As a method for instructing the human heart the retreatant's prayer explicitly banks on truth revealed in the incarnation. Bodily senses are the medium for experiencing a higher reality and power. This higher reality is a spiritual appropriation of heart-knowing in faith. Their bodily senses become spiritualized. Undergirding lies a theory of imagination and affections which asserts that any apprehension in prayer is rooted in sensibility. Only through sense experience can personal knowledge of being, God, and the world be received. Faith requires a fundamental sensory element. E. F. Schumacher informs the method:

> Everything in the world around us must be matched, as it were, with some sense, faculty or power within us; otherwise we remain unaware of its existence. There is therefore a hierarchic structure of gifts inside us, and not surprisingly, the higher the gift the more rarely it is to be found in a highly developed form, and the greater are the efforts required for its development.[4]

Regular praying over the biblical exterior Word of God in Jesus disposes the former retreatants to being sensibly embraced in faith. Through praying with and immersing themselves in Scripture, the interior Word of God, the indwelling Spirit is further awakened, energized, set in motion. Scripture unveils Jesus as the divine artist, revealing the art of loving. "All art is about God in the sense that all great works show the perplexed human being the path, the way up the mountain"[5] to Beauty, Life, Love. And the perplexing paradox that the retreatants experience is that their own bodily senses are the Creator's, Jesus' work of art (Eph. 2:10).

In each of the narrative's artistry, a primary image emerges as the interpersonal locale around which living faith is most focused. Each of these locales can be seen as fonts of grace, centers from which the living waters of God's consolations flow in the hearts of the former retreatants.

Emmett's postretreat experience portrays great sensible consolation still abiding around remaining in touch with the interior image of God as Abba, Father, holding Emmett as a son, with even more love than Emmett experiences while holding his own little boy. For Melissa the primary locale or graced image emblazoned inside her heart is nursing at Mary's breast as a baby. Sitting in an interior gaze with this portrait of herself gives Melissa a seat from which she receives empowerment within the gift of discerning spirits, protecting her from self-destructive tendencies in daily living. Arlena's story illuminates two self-portraits. One picture radiates truth, as it is accompanied by felt relief from angers, guilt, and shame. The second picture depicts her false self as it is accompanied by inner heartfelt movements connoting anxiety, timidity, and fear about facing pains residing within Arlena. Meditating upon a Gospel account of Jesus at Calvary powerfully evokes inner affections for Arlena, affections that receive the healing touch of Christ's immediate personal presence in faith. Paul's life experience following retreat, despite forgetfulness and sinfulness, shows us a heart continuing to carry and relate to yet another central image, his own fountain of healing grace. This image portrays himself as a baby son being held on the shoulder of God as Abba, Father.

Viewed as a portrait gallery wherein humanity and divinity intermingle, the illuminations evident in Emmett's, Melissa's, Arlena's, and Paul's narratives reveal multifaceted learnings and implications which enhance Christian living informing teachers and leaders of prayer. Indeed the first learning is seeing and naming Ignatian Trinitarian relating as synonymous with healing evangelical prayer. In other words, what becomes evident in simplicity through each of the retreatant's experiences of God, after having entered into the Ignatian interpersonal dynamic for praying, is a magnified showing of fundamental biblical spirituality. Entering into the mystery, the adventure of following Ignatius's Spiritual Exercises as a charted map for the human heart, takes each person to focus interior affections in an intensely concise fashion, while relating to biblical portraits of Jesus. The Spiritual Exercises can be described as an evangelical invitation to personally experience and appropriate revelation as living Beauty and Truth through praying with the Sacred Scriptures.

Jesus, as divine artist, when meditated upon and contemplated is Beauty, is Love, and as such he develops our higher faculties. A second lesson taught by the personalization of faith occurring in the former retreatants' lives is that to treasure Scripture for its literary beauty or moral truth is to miss the point in Christian evangelism and ministry itself. The divine artist reveals Beauty in Scripture "so as to dispose the heart with desire for going up the mountain, which is what we really wish to do but keep forgetting,... that we may continually return to our first intent."[6] As the retreatants' are enabled, through grace, to cultivate the higher powers within their human nature, they experience an appropriation of "the mind of Christ" (1 Cor. 2:14–16, Col. 3:12–17) in a living faith doing justice (James 2:14–26). This activity best indicates the teleology of Christian prayer.

A third learning becomes evident. In each narrative portrait an overarching spiritual movement within Christ's Spirit can be witnessed transpiring, a movement of grace that carries the individual believer into a new depth of communal relationships. Instead of personal freedom in faith being lived out in an increasingly self-reliant autonomy, we see each former retreatant being moved into living within a more connected relational posture with and for others. Paul finds himself participating in an adult faith-sharing group. More requests for mentoring others as a spiritual director occur. Arlena's relationship with her estranged husband becomes less abusive, more reflective of God's justice. Her ability to lead others to Christ as a public speaker and catechist dawns as Arlena experiences increasing inner strength and confidence. Melissa's whole capacity for making life-promoting decisions in the workplace expands. She struggles and becomes more able to take care of others from a nondysfunctional inner posture. Service for others becomes less rooted in her own fundamental fear of being abandoned. Melissa now invites others more fearlessly to prayerfully bring their pains and struggles to Jesus in the paschal mystery. She also experiences a newfound awareness of unjust social structures operating systematically to stifle the life-giving power of Jesus' Spirit in the world. Emmett ends up taking a public vow of nonviolence within deepening realizations of Abba's love amid his own mixed motives and human flaws. Emmett's pastoral leadership receives enabling grace not to give in to the tendency to take sides with conflicting factions in his congregation. By remaining Christ-centered in facing these conflicts, he helps bring about racial harmony where there had been a spirit of disunity.

These everyday narrative portraits of living faith doing justice illuminate the everyday mystical dynamic experienced in the Spiritual Exercises as naturally carrying the human heart into self-emptying communal relationships serving others. From personally experiencing and allowing grace to take root in their lives each former retreatant's life acts challengingly, carrying an impact upon societal institutions. Arlena's new life of grace renegotiates boundaries for what should be endured for the institution of marriage to remain viable. Emmett's vowed pacifism runs counter to the mind-set of our national and international military-industrial complex. Melissa's call to work free from a false sense of care-taking will challenge her colleagues' experience and on-the-job performance, inviting them not to work as counselors out of affectively disordered personal needs to be needed. Paul's receptivity to God's grace contributes to the Roman Catholic Church's understanding of the interdynamic between personal charism and institutional discipline regarding mandatory celibacy for priesthood.

Life itself becomes an art, a living divine drama for Arlena, Emmett, Melissa, and Paul. By apprehending Jesus as Beauty and Love, through imaginative praying in faith, the former retreatants relate to themselves, others, and the world in a mission of Christianizing relationships. This means allowing disordered affections, in ongoing prayer, to be ordered by Love, Jesus' Spirit.

Evelyn Underhill deserves to be quoted at length here. Her book *Practical Mysticism for Normal People* teaches contemplation, and in it I find an introduction to Ignatius Loyola's educational anthropology which explains and promises efficacy in the application of senses as a method for praying. She writes:

> Union represents not so much a rare and unimaginable operation as something which the practical person is doing in a vague, imperfect fashion, at every moment of his conscious life; and doing with intensity and thoroughness in all the more valid moments of life. We know a thing only by uniting with it; by assimilating it; by an interpenetration of it ourselves. It gives itself to us, just insofar as we give ourselves to it; and it is because our outflow toward things is usually so perfunctory and so languid, that our comprehension of things is so perfunctory and languid too.... Wisdom is the fruit of communion.... Because he has surrendered himself to it, the patriot knows his country, the artist knows the subject of his art, the lover his beloved, the saint his God.... Real knowledge always implies an intuitive taste.... True analytic thought follows swiftly upon the contact, the apprehension, the union.[7]

Experiencing God's affectionate regard for us is fundamental to Ignatius's educational methodology, emphasizing imaginative touch, sensate healing. C. S. Lewis in his essay "The Weight of Glory" explains in this play on words that the Hebrew meaning for "glory" is the weight of God's regard for us. Lewis invites Christian educators to teach that our life is a pilgrimage during which we are to enjoy the folly of trying to measure God's affectionate delight in us as daughters and sons. All Christian education must be rooted in a deepening faith that praises, reverences, and serves Christ as a result of entering into this affective folly, this "principle and foundation" (Sp. Ex. #23).

The imagination engaged in Christian prayer orders our affections as cognitive powers touch reality. Vital to mention here is that

the concept of affection designates a basic attunement which lies at the heart of a person's way of being and acting.... In quite specific ways, our affections qualify our perceptions, our fundamental attitudes and behavior; yet affections cannot be reduced to feelings, perceptions, or attitudes. Nor every affection is rooted in the center of one's self with equal force or comprehensiveness.[8]

Relying upon these insights pertaining to imaginative touch and the nonequal force of the varied human affections at work in the heart, a fourth intriguing learning unfolds spiritually, confirming some basic psychological theses underlying Alice Miller's book *The Drama of the Gifted Child*[9] and Robert Kegan's work *The Evolving Self*.[10] It becomes evident in three of the four transcripts that the center of one's self is being addressed by Christ's Spirit within images connoting "being held safely as a child by a loving gaze." Healing grace flows out from this medium in the heart's sensible imagination with an extra primal force, with authoritative love. More so than with other mediating images, being held as a child by Mary or God as Abba, Father, brings these former retreatants in contact with powerful consolations that shape and set in motion continual healing prayer (Rom. 8:14–28, Phil. 4:4–7). These consolations then lead to a multiplication of interior windows for receiving and experiencing grace. As a foundational principle for understanding how life in Christ is most efficaciously built up, the implication arises that the key to participating in Christ's deepest healing graces resides in one's willingness and ability to rest safely in prayer, contemplating as a child God's loving gaze. Such a foundational principle gives impetus for training leaders in the ministry of inner healing prayer. It gives added weight to the need for teaching and fostering contemplative living in the church.

A fifth implication draws upon what I will call the "being-held-by-God" principle. Scott Peck in his most recent book *Further Along the Road Less Traveled,* together with a small group of colleagues, are exploring diagnostic interplay between psychiatry and Christian spirituality. If deepening healing is essentially promoted by connecting a person's inner affective regard as a child with experiencing Christ's real presence holding us in love, then a clarion call needs to be heard. Psychiatric diagnostic insights need to study vigorously the efficacy of merging with theological diagnostic skills, most especially those contained in the theological educational anthropology of Ignatius Loyola's experiential guidelines for discerning interior heartfelt movements, spirits. This research need not be restricted to Christian therapists so long as one is willing to take an "at-risk" posture for research utilizing the twelve-step "higher power" approach. Already much has been studied through the twelve-step self-help movement; however, employing Ignatian insights would take us to a new and deeper level of mutual understanding. If therapists and pastoral counselors would become more able to discern healthy and unhealthy spiritual movements in persons' hearts by confronting and including spiritual dimensions of human experience, tremendous justice would be served. As Peck notes,

> Misdiagnosis almost inevitably results in mistreatment. But that is hardly the end of it, because mistreatment or inadequate treatment can occur in the face of a correct diagnosis. Indeed, my concern with misdiagnosis is relatively minor. A far greater problem, to my mind, has been the vast amount of mistreatment of patients with a correct primary diagnosis by virtue of psychiatry's neglect of and antipathy for spiritual issues.... The single most common complaint I hear from psychotherapy patients about their therapists has been that they did not or would not listen to the spiritual aspects of their lives.[11]

In each former retreatant's story an inner awareness of psychological pain becomes efficaciously participative in experiencing healing once God's gaze was felt. A person left in therapy with only a growing awareness of causative psychodynamics from family history, without a heartfelt connectedness to God's personal love, truncates real accessibility to Christ's healing power amid the major psychiatric advances discovered in this century. Therapists who dare to explore Ignatius Loyola's "application of senses" as a method for praying will enhance the wholistic health of their patients while informing theologians needing to apply their insights for the service of God's people. Suggested points of collegial interplay between current psychiatric insights and Ignatius Loyola's diagnostic understanding of the human person, inclusive of heartfelt spirits, can contribute to improving health services for the twenty-first century. Two such points for interweaving research are:

- a further differentiation between the human experiences of debilitating depression and/or a spiritual darkness connoting conversion and growth;

- studying the role and effects of persons interiorly exercising (or not exercising) the active principle of heartfelt gratitude, governing with a hierarchic creative force the other human affections.

Entry points that promise medical and theological diagnostic enrichment are numerous. These provide a beginning.

Continuing with the theme of each narrative revealing a portrait that instructs us, I turn to looking at points of inner resistance, points of unrelating with Christ's Spirit. Paul resists entering into a death of desire prayer, interpersonally surrendering and placing conflicting desires in Jesus' heart. When Paul does act in trust, following interior movements of consolation amid doubts, he experiences a grand freedom. He receives an appropriation of grace freeing him from fears surrounding physical death. Melissa feels an inner gagging or dissonance whenever she begins to resist relating to the world without being in an inner posture of allowing herself to be cared for by Mary, mediating God's love. Whenever she does say an interior "yes" to posturing her heart in a receiving mode, consolation flows. Painful situations at work become balanced. Arlena resists going to Jesus with pains and sufferings, only turning to Christ in the felt good times. When Arlena contemplates Calvary and allows her sufferings to be touched by Jesus' healing presence, new life, new energy emerges that strengthens her. Emmett resists allowing himself to be a happy mess of mixed human motives. When Emmett allows himself to be imperfect with Christ, he experiences God's loving him and working through his human flaws.

At each of these points of resistance a sixth simple learning is made evident. Once the fundamental desire awakens to grow closer to God, secure areas of the heart's ego strength will be gently, persistently addressed by Jesus' Spirit. This felt calling challenges ego strength to deepening spiritual strengths, moving the heart to break open in trustful reliant weakness on God's Spirit (2 Cor. 12:9–10). This calling forth addresses areas of the human heart, where health-producing ego strength resides, with all of its confidence and protective boundaries, to let go in relational acts of trusting by following the lead of Christ's Spirit. Beyond confidence each former retreatant is invited into doubts. Beyond protective defenses each is led into vulnerable reliance on God alone. The interior impulses of Christ's leading are always rooted in and accompanied by felt spiritual consolations that encourage natural growth rather than violate natural human developmental needs (Sp. Ex. #314, #315). In other words, our portraits of resistances in the former retreatants' hearts illuminate the fact that interpersonal spiritual relating with Christ always ends up leading ego strengths to a deeper dependent spiritual strength. The mind of Christ becomes appropriated and union becomes more heartfelt in each story as invitations from Jesus' Spirit are recognized, acknowledged, and responded to with generosity (Rom. 12:2). Whenever these invitations to "let-go and let-God" are not heeded, experiences of desolation make themselves evident in Paul's, Melissa's, Arlena's, and Emmett's stories (see Guidelines for the Discernment of Spirits, #322).

George Vaillant's *The Wisdom of the Ego*, James Fowler's *Stages of Faith*, and Robert Kegan's *The Evolving Self*, all significantly contribute to studying the dynamic process of human maturation. Answering the question of how we mature, Vaillant writes:

> Our advancements take place in relationships.... There has to be a relationship in which the child gets nurturance to proceed. Affective attachment plays the primary role.... Intellect rides on the back of affective bonding.... Mature defenses grow out of our brain's evolving capacity to master, assimilate, and feel grateful for life, living and experience. Such gratitude encompasses the capacity for wonder.... Not surprisingly ... the linking of idea and affect is an essential component of most

psychotherapies and self-help groups. And all of them help to foster the spiritual and psychological growth that sometimes help us to develop hope, faith and gratitude even late in life.[12]

Jesus as Love, the ground of all reality, indeed Reality Itself touches us in self-communication through all things.[13] While relating thoughts and emotions to God in prayer a circular revelation dawns and more Love is tasted as the imagination of each former retreatant learns to be exercised spiritually, affectively attaching itself to and interpenetrating the poverty and details of Christ's life. They come to experience affections harmonizing within, enabling them to see glimpses of God's hidden laboring in all things, loving us (Eph. 3:8–10, Sp. Ex. #230–37). "A pattern emerges too, of particular affections which constitutes and governs the life of the Christian."[14] Here a seventh implication is notable. If we allow imaginative powers to escape contemplating Jesus' concrete, incarnational realities, our humanity becomes guided by illusions that atrophy our sense of being. We may then be Christians in name, but our behaviors will manifest unfree, unloved affective being. Arlena's original flight from relating her pain to the details of Christ's passion narratives, as well as the overarching spiritual movement inside Emmett to embrace Jesus as contrasted to a generic God illuminate this point.

Analogical imagining, as taught by William Lynch in *Christ and Apollo,* describes a critical insight from Ignatian educational anthropology, an insight to attend to in the church's evangelism:

The analogical imagination insists on keeping the same and the different, the idea and the detail, tightly interlocked in the one imaginative act. As its idea or pattern descends into the images of reality, it adapts itself perfectly to every detail or difference, without ever suffering the loss of its own identity. And the theme is always on the inside of the images. It is always eminently positive and creating difference and autonomy.... Analogy means, ana—logan, "according to measure."[15]

In this theological educational anthropology, "imaginative powers, active in prayer, show faith (pistis) conferring insight and understanding (gnosis) into the mysterious object of faith, Jesus, Exterior Word, Beauty."[16] In short, meditating on incarnational details does not diminish our sensible and cognitive knowing. In fact, the more we prayerfully lose ourselves in attending to God's presence in the incarnational details of today, the more we find ourselves living the mysteries of Scripture (Luke 17:31–33). We attain the goal of Christian evangelism. We learn Christ's story as our own. And the measuring of Love breaks open the categories and scales of possibilities within (Mark 9:23). God does infinitely more in us and through us than we can ask or imagine (Eph. 3:20–21). The prevailing affective result in the former retreatants' hearts as they attended to relating to the biblical details of Christ's life is one of gratitude. Each narrative reveals a deepening sense of felt gratitude followed by a deepening desire to live immersed evermore in Christ's life.

In their Trinitarian praying, within the primary images emergent for each former retreatant, it becomes clear that these images correspond to a primary heartfelt wound. This eighth illuminated learning invites further pastoral diagnostic research. How much more speedily does healing occur if the believers consistently permit themselves to attend obediently to interior conversational prayer from within the heart's primary wound.

Paul carried an underlying fear of physical death, Melissa a fear of being abandoned. Both Arlena and Emmett suffered core physical and emotional abuse from childhood, handicapping their ability to believe themselves to be lovable. In all four persons, primary wounds meet with a surprisingly evocative image accompanied by their strongest felt consolations during their experience of the Spiritual Exercises. Foundational gratitude and joy then strengthen and shape their inner regard for themselves and the world at large.

Implied in this showing is a ninth lesson. It seems that the qualitative depth or extensiveness of a believer's healing is determined by "the extent that God's glory is recognized and worshipped."[17] The challenge for each former retreatant, each believer is to generously engage in seeking out and relating to hidden glory implicit in the external details of Jesus' life, especially those details that are accompanied by desolations around the believer's primary heartfelt needs. Each transcript teaches us that consolation, rendering joy and gratitude, increases even amid suffering the world in love, so long as one inwardly relates to Jesus' story as our story too, alive in the Holy Spirit. Desolations evoked reveal dimensions of the human heart which are love-sick, facets of the heart that are sick for love. A diminishing vulnerability to attack by the evil spirit transpires as the person courageously seeks for and worships God's hidden glory living in the heart's wounds.

It is the task of the person to appropriate interiorly what he or she perceives exteriorly in the history of God with his people. Christ's incarnation and paschal mystery have won the victory over the disruption caused by sin. Hence, it is both possible and necessary that the senses be healed, that the Christian acquire a taste for God which allows him to perceive God present in sensate realities.[18]

In the incredible mystery of the incarnation it must be recognized, however, that "hiddenness" itself is a personal characteristic of Jesus' life. Isaiah described the Savior as one who "had no form or come-liness that we should look at him, and no beauty that we should desire him" (Isa. 53:2).

That scriptural truth of Jesus' divinity being accompanied by the personal trait of "hiddenness" necessarily presents retreatants and all maturing believers with a tenth lesson. There is the need to ac-cept profound ambiguity and paradox as sources of healing grace. Because really, historically, Jesus is both attractive and too much for people (Mark 6:1–6), miraculously powerful yet uncondition-ally accepting of human weakness (Luke 2:8–20), visible yet hidden (Mark 3:11–12). Relational growth in the Holy Spirit requires a love of self and neighbor which embraces human limits, human needs for self-concealment, and human hungers for living amid hidden sacramental mystery which nourishes our spirits. St. Ignatius Loy-ola encouraged retreatants to taste and see God's hidden glory alive *in* Jesus' suffering love at the Calvary event. In our own Calvaries, we too are called to accept innocent suffering in redemptive loving, the antithesis of masochistic or self-inflicted suffering. In affectionate companionship with Jesus, St. Ignatius Loyola came to understand that we are forever invited participants in "the true nature of love wherein hiddenness becomes a condition for true ongoing experi-ences of revelation. Since love as compared with sheer power never does violence, the only way for Jesus as Love to reveal himself is through glory in self-concealment."[19] We participate in Jesus' vic-tory over violence in the world each time we freely, often hiddenly, choose to suffer with and for others in reconciling love. It is then that healing grace especially emanates from within us and Jesus' glory shines.

Chapter Six

MINISTRY AS HEALING, PRACTICAL MYSTICISM

Ministry as healing, practical mysticism speaks to people's expanding appetites for understanding and experiencing spiritual relationships. In a world starved by the one-dimensional way of knowing offered by the scientific method, this emphasis will prove itself more than useful as we approach the twenty-first century. Ministerial laboring as healing, practical mysticism will constructively nourish and feed the hungry (Matt. 25:34–35) while actively resisting the temptation to an otherworldly hyperspiritualism in this new age. Jesus' exhortation to "seek first the kingdom" (Matt. 6:33) can be wholeheartedly embraced in this focused interpersonal relating.

In their book *Megatrends 2000,* Patricia Aburdene and John Naisbitt assert that liberal new-agers and conservative fundamentalists share a common desire. Both are "seeking the same thing, a link between their everyday lives and the transcendent."[1] In mainline Protestant and Catholic churches the number of requests for spiritual counseling and spiritual direction continues to multiply, often beyond the capacities and number of trained religious leaders. Retreat movements, teaching various spiritualities, elicit increasing popularity. "We can see a new interest in the spiritual life all around us. We see a new insistence on its importance."[2]

In the United States, the mass media increasingly involves itself in appealing to the general public's hunger for discovering meaning in spiritual relationships. Centers for broadcasting and publishing houses that feature spirituality are multiplying, while reaping greater public attention and profits. In Latin America, Christian base communities grow rapidly in number, as dynamic gatherings blending prayer and political strategizing in spiritual-relational renewal. In China and Africa the church experiences burgeoning attendance. People in Eastern Europe and new states of the former Soviet Union couple their quests for human rights with this interest and desire for deepening religious expression. The evidence of people's increasing hunger for a food that lasts, in spiritual-relational living is superabundant. "To be sure, a profound truth is (re)emerging in this revival. The renewal of the spiritual life all around us arises primarily from our de facto situation. It is the concrete reality of our existence that poses the problem of the spiritual life once more."[3]

Webster's Dictionary defines "practical" as "exhibited in or obtained through practice and action." Ministry as healing, practical mysticism appropriates multidimensional, heartfelt knowing. This renders awe, purposefulness, and providential gratitude in the believer, as personal humility and poverty of spirit are accepted as relational gifts.

As a participant in ministry as healing, practical mysticism, the believer's heart must be engaged in more than intellectual assent. An affective single-mindedness actively practicing the biblical call for "seeking first the kingdom," with its preferential option for the poor, requires prayer and reflection in the everyday. Through this practice and activity, accompanied by communal reflection, we as believers discover links between everyday life and our hunger for God's transcendent loving presence among us. A Trinitarian theology of prayer and discernment of spirits, based on the tradition of the Spiritual Exercises of St. Ignatius Loyola, lies at the root of this ministerial identity. His is a living tradition in Christian spirituality, one recently rediscovered, bursting with potential adaptation to our present needs in the church.

This emphasis in ministry demonstrates its practicality in yet another sense. We are all born with the desire to receive and give love, regardless of economic background, gender identity, race, or ethnicity. Healing, practical mysticism works from within and through the contextuality of the believer. It is transcultural, ministerial service that liberates the human heart for greater loving, bringing social structures into a harmony that refracts the light of Jesus the Christ.

Is ministry as healing, practical mysticism just a synonym for that branch of theology called practical theology? The answer to this question is, "Yes, it is very related, but no, it is not the same." James Fowler, a recognized international church leader, writes extensively on the subject of practical theology. I turn to his working definition of that discipline in order to differentiate and clarify the meaning of ministry as healing, practical mysticism. Fowler writes in *Faith*

Development and Pastoral Care: "Practical Theology is theological reflection and construction arising out of and giving guidance to a community of faith in the praxis of its mission. Practical Theology is critical and constructive reflection leading to an on-going modification and development of the ways the Church shapes its life to be in partnership with God's work in the world."[4]

Healing, practical mysticism is this, and yet uniquely a model which asserts that *constructive partnership* with God directly depends upon knowing and discerning the initiatives intended by Christ's Spirit. This ministerial laboring takes us to distinguish which inner calls run counter to or are in greater harmony with the living Spirit of Jesus the Christ. In other words, this approach in ministry emphasizes prayer and discernment because they are far different from our accepted common understandings of rational reflection and construction. Healing, practical mysticism reminds church leaders and the people of God at large that, "If Yahweh does not build the house, in vain do the laborers labor" (Ps. 127).

It would be a serious misrepresentation to imply that Fowler's theological reflection is to be construed as merely rational. Much of his work promotes holistic reflection in the churches as an antidote for a truncated rational theological reflection in the tradition of the Enlightenment. For many, however, theological reflection translates as "think about" or "think over" as we decide what to do or what program to initiate in ministry. All too frequently we separate human freedom and understanding from already being in a heartfelt relationship with a living person who is the indwelling Spirit, and who is the Lord and Giver of Life. On this basis, Fowler's theological reflection in practical theology includes active imagination, sensual contemplation, and rational theory in heart-knowing. Ministry as healing, practical mysticism acts as a specialized focus to inform practical theology through an encouraged assurance. The assurance springs from a focusing upon affective, wholehearted reflection, liberated from a narrowed understanding of human reason and rationality. Analogously speaking, practical mysticism is the fuel that makes the fire of practical theology refract and burn with the healing light of Jesus' Spirit. This activity in contemplation does not separate human wisdom from the reality of God as our ground of being in the everyday. Rather, healing, practical mysticism actively focuses on the experience of gratitude amid ministerial call and our response to God's living work, in conversational partnership (John 15:16).

Practical mystics accept the theological truth of the *imago Dei* living within them. Ministers in this approach to co-laboring taste the possibility of praying always (1 Thess. 5:17) in the very posturing of their hearts. This ministerial model assumes God's nearness, the time being *now* to be awake to the movements of the Holy Spirit within us (Rom. 13:11–12, 5:5). There is also the assumption of God's eagerness to instruct us as friend and teacher (John 15:15, 16:7–15). Because we are each living images of Christ, this ministerial model proclaims boldly, the Holy Spirit as indwelling Word speaking through the inner affective movements of our hearts. The Word is found, felt, thought about, seen, and imaged by heart-knowing. For the practical mystic, inner affective movements of genuine consolation producing healing are not analogous to the voice of God. These inner movements address us as the Spirit's own promptings and whispers. The theology of prayer at work in this model of ministry is Trinitarian. Ministers live within this community of Persons as adopted daughters and sons, enjoying the promised fullness of inheritance (Gal. 4:5–7). Once recognized and heard, the daily inner touch and call of the Holy Spirit requires responses. In *The Church in the Power of the Spirit*, Jürgen Moltmann refers to the universal, historical intention of God at work in Christian proclamation when he writes, "It breaks into every situation as call and consolation.... It is not a neutral chronicle but the proclamation of God's decisive eschatological act of salvation."[5]

A very beautiful description of Trinitarian partnership for ministers as practical mystics is given by Moltmann. Describing the minister as listening, surrendering, and rejoicing in freedom, he writes:

What happens in the Son's self-offering on the cross is the revelation of the nature of God himself. In this happening God is revealed as the Trinitarian God, and in the event between the surrendering Father and the forsaken Son, God becomes so vast in the Spirit of self-offering that there is room for the whole world, the living and the dead.... And because the Father is reconciled to the world through the death of the Son, its new life must also serve the reconciliation of the world. Insofar as, with the epistle to the Hebrews, we can term Christ's sacrifice on the cross a priestly ministry, its consequence is the priesthood of all believers. They are all ambassadors of reconciliation in Christ's stead. They live in fellowship with God by virtue of Christ's giving of himself for them. Because of this their life is also destined for self-giving.[6]

Primarily then, ministry as healing, practical mysticism assures that our partnership with God's work in the world can be discerned. How often today do rational, reflective individuals or communities freely hear and choose to live in a biblical posture of self-sacrificial giving with a preferential option for serving the poor? How often do we assume Enlightenment categories of rational knowing and cut ourselves off from wholeheartedly hearing, receiving, and acting upon God's calling in our particular contexts? "The reign of God is not easy to discern. It demands both humility and active responsibility. The person's confrontation with the reign of God requires the person's active ability to undertake an active search for, to discern and to construct the particular realities that, at a given moment, appear to be the more likely to hasten or constitute the coming reign."[7] Very often today I see our people tragically separating themselves from the joy which accompanies receiving and responding to the Holy Spirit's inner voice. The disconnection between us and God's immediate presence, in part, stems from willful refusals to listen in prayer. Also however, there exists a great lack of simply knowing "how to" listen for the Holy Spirit's movements within, movements speaking and rendering energy for our partnership with the divine. Ministry as healing, practical mysticism intentionally enhances relational living with Christ's Spirit.

Mysticism often conjures up images of otherworldliness and rare spiritual powers. The mere mentioning of mysticism frequently moves our imaginations to think of strange shamans and psychics who peddle their spiritual insights, a guru in Tibet or St. Francis of Assisi speaking ecstatically with animals centuries ago. These images can engender awe. They also suggest a weirdness that commonly does not appeal to our real concrete need and desire for growing in wisdom and love. The images remain distant and ineffectual. They tend not to invite us to taste the immediacy of our own calling in Christ's Spirit and the glory of "praising, reverencing and serving God in everyday experience."[8]

Healing, practical mysticism takes believers to be very much in this world, presently working to integrate prayer within the marketplace, science, the arts, and politics. Mysticism properly understood

does connote spiritual power, a power not distant and rare, but readily accessible to the priesthood of all believers. Inner sight results
as one engages in true prayer. What is seen then, through a process of maturing, and in an expanding relationship with Jesus' Spirit,
is "God laboring in and through all things to love me, us."[9] This
ongoing vision in the present engenders an awe, admiration, and
gratitude that leads to an imitation of Christ's self-offering. Deep,
practical ecstasy is experienced in this relationship because of the
actual immediacy of the touch of Jesus' Spirit in us and for us.

What is a test of whether or not Christian prayer is authentic
and effectual in the heart of the believer? Isaiah the prophet speaks
clearly to us: "God is not impressed with the worship of Israel, with
vain offerings and incense, the 'calling of the assemblies': 'When you
spread forth your hands I will hide my eyes from you even though
you make many prayers, I will not listen: your hands are full of
blood' (Isa. 1:15)."[10] People must listen to the call of the Spirit and
cease doing evil, learning to do good. "Seek justice, correct oppression; defend the fatherless, plead for the widow" (Isa. 1:17). True
prayer must be accompanied by growing personal freedom that enjoys "peace, self-control, gentleness, patience and kindness" (Gal.
5:22). This always employs the Christian in service with and for
others. The quality of this service directly relates to the acceptance
of one's own real poverty in the Spirit. "Christian spirituality is the
spirituality of the poor man of Nazareth who took upon himself the
form of a servant. To know God is to do justice and plead the cause
of the oppressed: to know God in Christ is to share in his work
of establishing justice in the earth, and to share in his poverty and
oppression."[11]

True prayer then is evident through the believer's expanding capacities to receive and give love, "healing" connoting an enlarging of
the person's heart to feel with Christ's Heart in partnership (2 Cor.
6:11–18), in practical, relational living. Signs of real growth include
virtuous acts of service for others, especially the poor, an increasing
acceptance of one's own powerlessness, and the fruits of the Holy
Spirit. The taming of compulsions and aggressions will be evident
in the renewal of our personalities and our minds, "as we put on
the new self that has been created in God's way" (Eph. 4:23). Always too, true prayer heals, bettering a person's capacity to live on
in the experience of freedom. Jürgen Moltmann writes: "The exuberance of freedom is depicted and anticipated in the exuberance

of ecstasy.... The feast of freedom is itself the festal celebration of life. For a particular time, in a particular space, through a particular community, the laws and compulsions of this world become invalid."[12]

Ministry as healing, practical mysticism participates in partnership with God, depending upon the minister's willingness to receive and respond to the Master's teaching (Matt. 23:10–12). "Seeking first the kingdom of God" implicitly readies us to learn how to fight single-mindedly for freedom from worldly compulsions in our present specific contexts. These compulsions subtly act to control our hearts as individuals and as social participants in unjust structures. The battle's subtlety demands sensitive discernment and practical mystical prayer. So that the practice of prayer and discernment does not turn into a spirituality of self-centered, individualistic pursuits for self-actualization, Ignatius Loyola vitally asserts the truth of a meditative reflection called "The Two Standards" (Sp. Ex. #136). In the fabric of this awareness, part of the fabric of Ignatius's daily examination of consciousness, we recognize and taste the battle between the Holy Spirit's invitations to live in harmony with all that is good and human and the evil spirit's promotions of disharmony and enslavement, as the enemies of human nature. St. Ignatius Loyola's living tradition teaches us that a "practical commitment to justice is *the* criterion for determining the authenticity of any form of mysticism that claims to be Christian, for prayer is 'the attitude one takes toward evil powers.' "[13] Practical mystics taste, through daily healing prayer, the "revelation that we are not in control, that we must risk daily abandonment as the cross becomes the seedbed in which genuine prayer grows."[14]

The real possibility of ongoing felt hope is experienced at the cross, in God's Spirit. Its exuberance defies worldly oppression, every day, in a prayerful relationship with Jesus. Mysticism today is generally defined through the ordinary lens of the scientific method. This places us in a real disadvantage within these Enlightenment categories of knowing. Such categories emphasize the primacy of reason according to empirical sciences whose "orientation toward *control* over nature achieve their desired objectivity through acquiring a certain *distance* from the object under analysis. But these two notions of *control* and *distance* are basically irreconcilable with the religious experience of God, because that experience hinges on *letting-go* and on *drawing near.*"[15] Within modernity's popular definitions, mysticism is rare and distant from ordinary life experience, besides being suspect.

A biblically accurate understanding names mysticism as our "consciousness of the experience of uncreated grace as revelation and self-communication of the triune God."[16] This working definition carries an implicit set of assumptions, the first of which is that mysticism is accessible to everyone who can consciously seek after God's presence-with-us. This openness to everyone compares with "the Christian receiving in the Creed, a personal understanding from God which tells us what we are and who we are to become."[17] It also carries the working assumptions that "we can experience ourselves as being constantly addressed by God. For God communicates and discloses himself in a very intimate way to the spiritual being of the person, drawing the whole world of man."[18] This drawing enraptures the practical mystic in the very heart of God. The free, near, accessibility of God's presence toward us, desiring to communicate to us, requires everyday responses in faith. Examples of living practical mystics include Helen Alvaré (director of the National Conference of Catholic Bishops' Pro-Life Activities), Charles Colson (founder of Prison Fellowship Ministries), Sr. Mary Rose Grady, D.C. (president of Covenant House serving runaway and homeless youth), and Jean Vanier (founder of the worldwide L'Arche communities serving the mentally handicapped). By listening and responding in and through a discipline of prayerful discernment, Jesus' Spirit teaches them and their co-workers effective strategies in the battle for enhanced spiritual-relational living. Practical mysticism ascribes the person in ministry to a way of being that brings about a greater interior freedom in the person's heart. This freedom conjoins us with the living biblical preferences existing in Christ's Heart.

The Hebrew meaning of "heart" is the center of the person, where reason, emotions, and will all act in harmonious spiritual knowing. "Hans Walter Wolff notes that the most important word in the vocabulary of Hebrew Biblical anthropology generally translates as 'heart.' It occurs 858 times in the Hebrew Bible."[19] Heart is expressed as the depth of one's desires, the source for feelings and temperament, the catalyst for understanding and insight. "The heart is our origin of ethical judgment, and the description of one's very self. In all of these interpretable frames, the heart surfaces as the essential aspect of personhood."[20]

Karl Rahner captures most profoundly the nature of the word

"heart." Rahner notes that the word is an *Urwort*, which best translates as a source or primordial word. An *Urwort* is rooted in multiple understandings and numerous layers of meaning. Such words are highly evocative, threaded with nuances and pregnant with inexhaustible depth. Central for Rahner is the capacity for the "heart" to define at the most fundamental level one's very personhood. "Heart" for Rahner, portrays the core experience of who we are as human beings.[21]

Ministry as healing, practical mysticism notes that one aspect of the heart's activity can be overemphasized such as thinking, feeling, or willing. But all of the dimensions of the heart's activity inform each other, rendering us aware of fundamental, interior, affective movements *that speak*. Which interior movements are sourced in the ongoing call and friendship of the living Spirit of Jesus is matter for day-to-day discernment. Amid praxis, a process of discernment essentially makes ministry effectual in the world. The biblical root meaning of "heart" assumes and acknowledges, in a faith relationship, our possession of the natural ability to "seek God in the hope that we might feel after him and find him" (Acts 17:27).

Christian mysticism springs from finding God's activity at work in our hearts and in the events around us in the world. Practical mystics announce with their lives what they see and experience, that the "kingdom of God is among us" (Luke 17:21), that "there is no need to be afraid because it has pleased your Father to give you the kingdom" (Luke 12:32). In finding this personal truth we are found. The parable of the pearl of great price carries a new inverted meaning. As we let go and taste the nearness of God's Spirit, we taste and see Christ's Spirit pursuing us, seeking us out, then spending everything for us (Matt. 18:44–46). Such loving, in allowing Scripture to reveal multidimensional meanings in a praying heart, heals compulsions, frees us from sinful patterns of Pelagian[22] behavior, and anoints inner desiring. We naturally are found, wanting to return love through committed loyalty in friendship with Jesus, at the foot of the cross.

Many find the words "practical" and "mystical" to be oxymoronic. I may be accused of creating my own definitions. Neither is true. These definitions are biblically grounded. They reflect a living theological tradition in the church. Today we are rediscovering multidimensional human knowing, both in conjunction with, and apart from, the epistemological categories operative since the Enlightenment. Methods of theological inquiry and research inclusively appreciate aesthetic and narrative approaches to human understanding. The religious experience of God's presence as indwelling Word is mysticism pure and simple. Partially, daily, seeing God's activity loving us, and feeling after God in faith, brings familiarity in relationship. Following the leads of the intending touch of Jesus' Spirit is a very real everyday mysticism, quite accessible to anyone willing and able to seek (Matt. 7:7–8).

The wholehearted embracing of Jesus' exhortation to "seek first the kingdom of God" enraptures the minister as practical mystic, so much so that we will even die for this relationship. For the relationship is the kingdom that we so ardently seek and long for in loving. "The kingdom of God, that Jesus is talking about is in this world through Jesus, himself."[23] The relationship with all things and persons in and through this primary relationship with Jesus' Spirit, acts, bringing about a process of "making our personal joy more complete" (John 15:11). Practical mysticism, rather than being oxymoronic, speaks about the ordinary ability in the human heart to find God and to fall in love. Pedro Arrupe, steeped in the spirituality of discernment as found in the *Spiritual Exercises* of Ignatius Loyola, writes:

> Nothing is more practical than finding God, i.e., than falling in love in a quite absolute, final way. What you are in love with, what seizes your imagination, will affect everything. It will decide what will get you out of bed in the morning, what you do with your evenings, how you spend your weekends, what you read, who you know, what breaks your heart, and what amazes you with joy and gratitude. Fall in love, stay in love, and it will determine everything.[24]

The seeking for a link between everyday living and the transcendent that new-agers and fundamentalists share is natural to us. Our hearts are made to be in love, to live in God who is Love (1 John 4:7–8).

Danger arises when human seeking for spiritual-relational meaning is disconnected or separated from the activity of Jesus' Spirit continually humbling himself, "not counting equality with God something to be grasped" (Phil. 2:5–11). Heartfelt disconnectedness from relating to Christ's Spirit easily results in the development of fear-filled personal and congregational rigidity, anticommunal nar-

cissism, or crippling gnosticism, isolating individuals from accountability in relationships. Other spiritual maladies readily debilitate
the human heart if closed off from listening for Christ's Spirit at
work in the world. Because we are made for love, who or what we
embrace most single-mindedly does determine everything. The insa-
tiable human spiritual hunger for a food that satisfies, in feeding off
of a relationship with Jesus' Spirit, finds the living bread come down
from heaven. As believers we experience healing, tasting increasing
life in expanding personal freedom, a life lasting forever (John 6:51)!

Chapter Seven

EVERYDAY PRAYER AND DISCERNMENT

The tool for everyday prayer and discernment, being gradually recovered in the living traditions of Ignatius Loyola, is the "examination of consciousness," a microcosm of inner dynamics at work in the Spiritual Exercises. The spiritual dynamism experienced when employing this prayer tool actively sustains graces received during Ignatius's Spiritual Exercises. A former retreatant also becomes propelled forward into relating with God's future through regularly engaging in this heartfelt way for praying. If this manner of praying is habituated in the heartfelt knowing of the believer, the practice of living in ministry as healing, practical mysticism becomes appropriated in our experience. Moreover, through people remaining faithful to practicing the examination of consciousness, wide-ranging communal benefits emerge. Whether gifted in ministry as apostles, prophets, teachers, healers, speakers of tongues, or administrators in the body of Christ, the church (1 Cor. 12:27–31), all become more effective participants in furthering the future coming of the kingdom. The grace of God, working through this prayer tool, promises ongoing tastes of hope, as well as ongoing conversion in the heart.

Practicing the examination of consciousness allows the human heart to be engaged in the awareness of God's indwelling presence speaking in and through our interior affective movements. Ministry as healing, practical mysticism critically depends upon the efficaciousness of this manner of praying. "The Examen" acts, dynamically preparing the heart for a deepening experience of God's loving presence through the *Spiritual Exercises*. And, for those who have made this retreat, it cultivates and keeps alive the "theologal"[1] of that experience in faith. For this reason a description of its relational characteristics is especially pertinent. Jon Sobrino writes in *Spirituality of Liberation*, "What is at stake in Spiritual Theology, is the actualization of primordial tautology that theology be a *word that speaks*' — this is, a word with a spirit of its own. It is not enough merely to speak of God. Theology must allow God to speak. Theology must relate the human being with God."[2] The examen of consciousness provides a real means for listening to God speak. To practice it is to taste kinship within the Trinity's life. Through a daily practicing of discernment, in our concrete circumstances, we realize our identities in Christ as the Spirit's actual living words!

The examination of consciousness is brief, intensive, and biblically based prayer. The foundational aspects are evident in Genesis. During the temptations of Adam and Eve in the garden, spiritual voices address them for good and for evil purposes. In the New Testament we see Jesus tempted in the desert. These temptations also haunt us. The examen of consciousness acknowledges the fact that we, like the old Adam and new Adam (Rom. 5:15–17) experience two fundamental spontaneities at work in our hearts. Jesus' temptations in the desert (Luke 4:1–13) illustrates the spontaneous experience of an antihuman voice, an affective word, that lures us to live out of a prideful grasping for power and honor. The other spontaneous call, that of the Holy Spirit, renders courage and wisdom to accept the glory and goodness of our humanity, human limits included:

> Put simply, two spontaneities well-up in the consciousness and experience of each of us. One is good and for God, another evil and not for God. For one who is eager to seek after God, to seek first the kingdom with his or her whole being, the challenge is to sift out these various spontaneous urges and impulses, and give full existential ratification to those spontaneous feelings that are from and for God. We do this by allowing the truly Spiritual spontaneity to happen in our daily lives.[3]

Through practicing the consciousness examen, a believer's heart is actualized for service as a contemplative-in-action. Categories that prevent laity and clergy alike from a deepening participation in ministry fall away in the "theologal" of this examen. Historically, all true prayer enkindles the fire of Christ's loving in the churches. A new quality of warmth and brightness is experienced.

The "how to" of the examen of consciousness requires entering into a commitment. Two fifteen-minute periods must be set aside each day. These periods should be at two different intervals of the day, for example, once after lunch and another early in the evening.

But the actual time intervals are fluid, depending upon the healing rhythms in the practical mystic's heart and depending upon the
circumstantial demands of any given day. These poignant prayer
events are entered into by allowing our hearts to become focused.
Attending to the ability to place oneself in an inner posture of
silent recollection, awakening the mind and senses, will yield fruit
in-the-Spirit.

The starting point for the practical mystic, in allowing oneself to
experience the healing guidance of the Holy Spirit, is one's own identity, in Christ. As living images of Christ, we stand before the Father,
in the power of the living Holy Spirit. We actively listen and respond
in faith, trusting in God's desire to communicate with us, not only
sustaining us by love in the present, but desiring to breed love in and
through us as the Holy Spirit indwells (John 17:26). As co-laborers
furthering the kingdom of God, we practice the consciousness examen within the precariously joyful truth of being commissioned
(John 15:16–17). And within the covenant promises we anticipate
seeing even greater things in the future of God's relationship toward
us (John 1:50).

At first the actual process of praying the examination of consciousness feels awkward and/or overly structured. This is to be
expected. Yet a self-forgetful dynamic develops as the practical mystic gives himself or herself to the encounter. Learning to dance is a
good analogy. Awkwardness leaves as we acquire familiarity with a
style of dancing, so too in this framework of praying, while exercising the human spirit. Regularizing this practice activates a sense of
real dynamism in our faith relationship with God.

The Spirit's presence is assumed in faith by virtue of our baptism
and the New Testament promises proclaiming the Advocate's willingness to teach us (John 16:13–15). As we attend to listening for
the music, the inner affective words or movements of the heart, we
thank and praise, petition, survey our inner affections, confess, and
make amendment in heartfelt hope. Like a dance, this prayer exercise
always depends upon our inner willingness to posture our bodies and
spirits in a way that notices the activity of the One leading us, giving
the Holy Spirit free reign. The prayer leads us spiritually into healing,
accepting more love, while experiencing being propelled into giving
more love to others.

The activity of God, always addressing our inner heart affectively, is noticeable. The brilliance of Ignatius Loyola's insight into

the workings of human affections is his asserting that Christ's Spirit moves in traceable stirrings of consolation in the human heart. This is always true unless the believer has committed grave sin (Sp. Ex. #314–15). Grave sinning must first be confessed, and forgiveness received, to allow inner consolations to lead and guide during affective assessments. The Ignatian tradition experiences and proclaims our God to be the seat and Lord of consolation. Christ's Spirit always leads to deepening consolations in faith.

Consolation is a general fundamental category for interior affective movements in Ignatian spirituality. It has as many names as there are experiences of consolation in life. Some synonyms and derivatives for inner affective consolations are gentleness, relief, calm, increasing hope and charity, and soothing joy (Sp. Ex. #316). Tears dissipating sadness are also included. The point here is that "consolation is a sign of progress and guidance from God, the Indwelling Holy Spirit" (Sp. Ex. #318–19). Ignatian theological anthropology also conveys the experienced truth of a second encompassing category describing heartfelt affective movements. This is the fundamental inner experience of *desolation*. Primary examples of affective movements in this category include sadness, melancholy, agitation, diminishing hope and charity, and anxiety (Sp. Ex. #317). These experiential movements never point to the Holy Spirit's urgings. "In desolation the evil spirit, the enemy of human nature, guides, lures and counsels the heart" (Sp. Ex. #6).

In practicing the examination of consciousness the practical mystic can daily enter into the foundational dynamics of the Spiritual Exercises, and be attuned to the healing urgings and loving of Jesus' intimate Spirit. The consciousness examen is not an activity that we take charge of and perform for self-perfection. It requires accepting as best we can an attitude of lowliness in true creaturehood, our absolute need for and dependence on God. This posturing in humility feels kinship with Mary in her magnificat as she expresses her soul magnifying the Lord, being exulted (Luke 1:46–47). In fact, the examen acts as a magnifying lens and helps us to see and "feel after God" (Acts 17:27) in the hope that we might respond generously like Mary: "Yes, let it be done to me according to your will" (Luke 1:38). Through using the consciousness examen we are brought into conflict with anti-Christian cynicism about the world and anti-Christian complacency for the lonely and poor who are suffering. All this progressively happens in the framework of daily discernment, everyday

mysticism. In and through our personal contexts of suffering and resurrection, we are daily confronted by God's living affective Word
within, requiring us to die to self-willfulness in loving service of
others (Luke 9:23–25).

Ministry as healing, practical mysticism specifically engages the
dynamism and discipline of two fifteen-minute prayer periods in
this manner. First, there is an *asking* for the light of the Holy
Spirit to guide and illuminate the experiences of affective movements
inside, where God has been speaking to us. This asking acknowledges our need to let go of tendencies leading us into disconnected
introspection, away from the Holy Spirit's presence.

Second, there is an inner leap of trust in *actively thanking* God
for being present in the day's experiences. This very much relates to
the first part. The depth and quality of this thanksgiving is possible
insofar as we permit ourselves to assume "the stance of a Christian,
that of a poor person, possessing nothing, not even himself, and yet
being gifted at every instant in and through everything as gift."[4]

Third, this manner of praying includes an *assessment of our inner
experiences* that day, in faith. This is not an analysis. Emphatically,
it is also not an *examination of conscience* evaluating our behavior.
To engage in a mindful exercise of grading behavior as good or bad,
desirable or less than desirable, runs contrary to the efficacy of the
consciousness examen. In this part of the dynamic listening in prayer,
the practical mystic attends to and surveys heartfelt, inner, affective
movements. Allowing ourselves to be recollecting, we recall and feel
again the consolations or felt drawings toward consolations, which
are God's voice speaking in the particularities of the day. This recollection involves, too, a trusting that God desires to speak plainly
(John 16:23–33). There is no need for much inner striving to remember events and feelings. The heart rests in a relaxed focusing
of the memory on what has been presenting itself to our consciousness. "The operative questions are: What has been happening in our
hearts, how has the Lord been working in us, what has the Spirit
been asking us? Again, interior moods, feelings, urges and movements are the 'spirits' that must be sifted out, discerned so we can
recognize the Lord's call to us in the intimate core of our being. Only
secondarily are our own actions to be considered."[5]

Fourth, the examen's dynamic carries the person at prayer to *feel
sorrow and contrition*. What flows from the affective assessment and
refeeling with God's encountered words inside our hearts is a natu-

ral sorrow. This sorrow carries no sense of destructive recrimination; rather this sorrow simultaneously tastes real mercy. I say naturally felt because of the infinity of God's justice and mercy rooted in love (1 John 4:8). "When we experience being extravagantly loved by the Spirit addressing us, desiring every ounce of our being, our own response is naturally less than adequate."[6] The quality of God's loving, always greater than our weak attempts, causes "sorrow naturally to spring from our lack of courage and honesty in responding to the mightiness of God's drawing us, calling us into a Heart that suffers with and serves others."[7] The direct result of this deepening grace in our consciousness is the proliferation of the good news by a personal testimony of loving through deeds more than mere speech (Sp. Ex. #230). The practice and experience of this part of the consciousness examen teaches the lesson that "they who have experienced God's mercy and forgiveness will be most understanding with the poor. When it is grasped that God is love, and love alone, practical mystics will seek the liberation of the poor with more disinterestedness and more effectiveness."[8] Healing radiates into the world from this manner of spiritual-relational living.

Fifth, the examination of consciousness concludes by the practitioner experiencing an interior invitation to *amend and resolve to respond* to the indwelling Spirit with greater faith and charity in the future. This too is a natural affective movement that carries the praying person to taste the desire to allow oneself to be more disposed to God's presence in the everyday. Being drawn to want to be more attentive to God's inner word, this faith relationship informs our questions and fashions our approaches to decision-making. This fifteen-minute focusing in our consciousness energizes us. A felt hope accompanies its praxis, a hope that can know peace beyond all understanding (Phil. 4:7) regardless of our plight. Through this final part of the consciousness examen "a sense of the nearness of God is translated into hope for the historical present. It is a type of hoping against hope (Rom. 4:18) because the historical future is obscure and because the misery is so great for so many in the present."[9]

In our hearts, where intellect, will, and emotion all live in congruence with our human spirit, God's Word speaks in and through our affective, heartfelt movements in kinship with Abba's Spirit. It is heart-to-Heart, spirit-to-Spirit communion in familial conversation. The Enlightenment's epistemological categories for a particular type of scientific methodology do not apply here. They cannot validate the practical nature of the experience received as we make a series of consciousness examens. Healing, practical mysticism will seem impractical, for the Spirit of Jesus inevitably leads beyond the reasonableness dictated by hard measurable data, in favoring apostolic initiatives involving vulnerable risks (e.g., saying yes to the Holy Spirit's call to open parish thrift shops for the inner-city poor in spite of crime rates pointing to probable theft; working with the sick in high-risk contagious environments; giving birth to or adopting severely handicapped children, etc.).

The theological anthropology of Ignatius Loyola and his companions in our century, Karl Rahner and Jon Sobrino, teaches ministry as healing, practical mysticism and provides this ministry with a foundation. It is a theological mysticism that is supported by "the whole of Sacred Scripture when we recall the element of human causality in the production of the various books. God personally created us in such a way that the Spirit might be the ground of our being, communicating personally to us, in our experience. God discloses His message progressively, maintains it, and manifests his intimate presence at various times and in many ways (Heb. 1:1)."[10]

In ministry as healing, practical mysticism, the daily practicing of the examination of consciousness is (amid many effective ways of being in touch with God's inner Word) the primary tool that enables prayer and discernment to actually take place in the heart of the individual Christian and in the Christian community. It is a methodology for praying that "concretizes to some extent, the personal experience of God."[11] The five moments of prayer in the dynamic structure of the consciousness examen are just that, dynamic. This means that all five moments are not experienced during each period of prayer. The practical mystic, pausing to attend to focusing on God's healing inner Word, may only experience the first and second parts of the examen, dancing inwardly in praise and thanksgiving on a given day. All five parts may be experienced on a different occasion. Again, the analogy of dancing appropriately conveys the posture that the praying person needs to assume. If God's Spirit is leading, just as in dancing, we will not take control of these moments of contemplation. We will listen for, notice, and respond to the experience of God's movements, "a word to be heard, and will to be complied with, a person to be trusted."[12] To experience ministerial laboring as healing, practical mysticism through committing oneself to practicing the consciousness examen is "to experience a daily invitation to discern our duty and not simply to deduce it from universal principles. It is an experience that informs practical theologians that the foundation of reality is not only some sort of 'reality in depth,' but reality as personal, reality as 'someone,' a someone who calls us, a someone whose concrete will must be complied with."[13]

The ecclesiology that emerges from the present-day historical experience of ministry as healing, practical mysticism continues the growth of living tradition in the church. This ecclesiology emphasizes the immediacy of familial, Trinitarian kinship in the everyday. "The term *ekklesia* as used in the New Testament is an eschatological term. It means an assembly or con-vocation and more specifically the convocation of the saints that will be realized at the eschaton."[14]

The church from this angle of vision is a family of practical mystics in the Pauline understanding of saints. It includes all living believers who daily struggle in this world to prayerfully seek first a relationship with Christ's Spirit, the living kingdom of love. The church also includes the living saints who have passed through death as an exit to ultimate communion within the family of the Trinity. These spiritual friends are Christian family members of the one Mystical Body of Christ that is the church (Rom. 12:4–5).

Practical mysticism views and experiences the church as "a mystical communion of men and women with each other, in Christ. This communion begins here on earth and reaches consummation in heaven. This implies that the church which exists inchoately in this life reaches fullness in the life beyond. Along with many Biblical authors the church is understood here as being within history as a foretaste or anticipation of what the church is to be."[15] Ordinary believers, saints on earth, are placed in spiritual relationships with saints on the other side of death's door. Prayer unites us all in intercession, mediating and reconciling, as living images of Christ. Abba's love for the world, in the power of the Spirit, addresses the world through living words, the practitioners of healing, practical mysticism. Prayer propels us into furthering the coming kingdom.

Quietly, hiddenly, as leaven works in bread, the minister as practical mystic labors in the world (Matt. 13:33). Prayer and discernment are hidden activities in the human heart, yet they carry an amazing energy creating, healing, and fashioning the human community. "According to Hippolytus the Risen Christ is the 'leader of the mystic round dance' and the church is the bride who dances with him."[16] The primary work of the church in our being commissioned to baptize all nations (Matt. 28:16–20) and to spread the good news is teaching prayer. To baptize in the name of the Father, Son, and Holy Spirit commits the church publicly to immersing people's hearts in Trinitarian relationships, in furthering the coming kingdom. And in this mission the consciousness examen takes on heightened importance. Along with other prayer tools that focus the human heart to hear and respond to God's indwelling Word, "the Examen" becomes a centerpiece for praxis in efficacious ministry.

Practical mystics elicit attention because their lives illustrate the direction and power of real prayer in Christian loving (e.g., Helen Alvaré, Charles Colson, Sr. Mary Rose Grady, D.C., and Jean Vanier). These men and women all publicly live in a manner that feasts on a regularized prayerful relationship with the living Spirit of Christ, their Bread of Life. And they all speak openly about that personal, spiritual relating as a food that satisfies. Each of their labors carries an acceptance of the necessity of struggle and the nobility of human suffering with and for others. Theirs is a radiant, warm, and contagious joy. Each experiences being elected by the Holy Spirit to lead a life full of grace. Because these men and women are discerning between the spontaneous, affective, and spiritual movements within their hearts, and because they are responding to those movements which are from God and for Christ's Spirit, actual potentialities in furthering God's kingdom are creatively being made real. Their lives, through the hidden leaven of prayer, become a bread that multiplies hope and nourishes the human spirit in and for loving. Spiritual-relational living truly provides alternatives to social complacency, fear-filled political paralysis, self-recrimination, and cynicism. Using Jürgen Moltmann's words, we can see in the life of the practical mystic that ministry as

> an alternative emerges and is presented in festal terms. This feast always means first of all that a community is freed from every compulsion and arrives at the spontaneous expression of its feelings, spontaneous ideas and spontaneous bodily movements. The liberating feast of the resurrection cannot be without euphoria. But it is not simply rousing a passing euphoria when it seizes men in the heart of this oppression and, with the freedom they celebrate, wakes their hunger for freedom; when it meets men in their suppressed feelings of loneliness and through the fellowship they celebrate wakes their cry for

the other person. Then the liberating feast radiates into everyday life a remembrance which cannot be forgotten again in the
daily round. It works as an antitype to normal standardized life
and lets us seek for possible ways of changing it. The liberating feast builds up a tension toward life in this world which
can only be resolved through conscious suffering over its lack
of freedom and through conscious intervention for more freedom and more open fellowship. If the feast of freedom is itself
celebrated as a liberating feast then it takes on the character of
anticipation. It is anticipated in song, in laughter, in play and in
dance.[17]

Chapter Eight

VON BALTHASAR'S
TRINITARIAN THEOLOGY
AND IGNATIAN PRAYER

I have experienced Hans Urs von Balthasar's Trinitarian theology as intimately compelling ever since I was first introduced to his inspirational writings. My ordination retreat, made at Gloucester, Massachusetts, in the spring of 1985, was the place of introduction. Life has not been the same since. Through the drawing power of von Balthasar's prose, I, like many, have been seized by the Father's mysterious beauty found at the foot of Jesus' grotesque cross, in the power of the Spirit. A small, personal apprehension of what von Balthasar sees as God's glory occurred during that retreat. This tidbit of spiritual apprehension became a grounding, yielding the "inspirational stuff" of my first homily as a Catholic priest. His book *Heart of the World* was prayed with during that particular period of retreat set aside for Ignatian prayer. This medium provided the substance for meditation and contemplation. What von Balthasar conveys about Calvary in the work drew me and draws me into an accessible, retrievable *sense* of my communion within Trinitarian loving. This "tasting" propels me through an energy (generated amid interior tears) to make some sense of suffering, with an overabundant confidence in the Father's will never to abandon me. More than those of any other theologian, von Balthasar's writings take me to God, leaving me simultaneously sober and inebriated, always thirsting for a deeper Trinitarian communion by concretely embracing the world in love.

An attempt at explaining von Balthasar's theology of the Trinity follows with a variety of quotations from his work simply entitled *Prayer*. Two scholarly articles are heavily relied upon. Let me begin the presentation of this overview from the perspective of standing with Jesus at Calvary, in all that indescribable wrenching disillusionment and sorrow. The cruel, cynical joke often voiced among common folk when bearing sufferings sounds something like this: "Well (making reference to the Calvary event), if that is how the Father treated his only Son, what should we expect?" Easily, this cynicism can fester in practiced, concrete experiences of Calvaries that we all live through, unless we receive the certain heartfelt knowledge that Jesus was and is never abandoned by the Father's love.

What kind of Father affirms his Son at the Jordan, through the depths of the Spirit speaking eternal delight (Matt. 3:17), only to desert his Son in the hour when Jesus needs him most? Does our walk in faith take us finally to a radical, individual event of aloneness in which we pay a cruel price within a *dislocated* promise? Is our rising in glory, somehow a *relocating,* a reconnecting in a new spiritual communion with the Father? If the answer in faith is "yes," then we are called to live with the terror that, finally, the Father's love which we regularly experience in prayer will not be mercifully present in our hour of greatest need. The Father who abandons us, as he did Jesus, will eventually send his Holy Spirit, and then reaffirm us in resurrecting from death. We need only wait in terror and trust.

Von Balthasar's theology of the Trinity adamantly rejects such ruminating and carries us into the awesome, mysterious truth that "Christ, the Father's Word-made-flesh, is both things at once."[1] This means that when Jesus cries out "Eli, la' ma sabach-tha'-ni? — My God, my God, why have you forsaken me?" (Matt. 27:46), he is experiencing *the* darkest night of the soul. Simultaneously, the Father is so intimately present, closer even than Jesus' breath, that this is the Father, one with Jesus, on the cross, crying out to the world, in the breath of the Spirit on Jesus' lips, "My God, my God, why have you rejected me." The Calvary scene in Scripture reveals what our Father is like. He never abandons his Son (or us as images of his Son). The Father remains faithful, crying out with the Son in utter oneness, through the mission of the Holy Spirit to the world.

> Jesus at Calvary, as well as at all other times and places, is the exegesis of the Father. At every moment he comes from the Father, not in the sense of the memory of a distant past but of a present actuality. At the same time, in every action he is going back to the Father. His destiny is not only to reveal the Father

to the world but to lead believers to participate in his Trinitarian being. As von Balthasar puts it, "By his prayer and his suffering, the Son brings his disciples — and through them, all mankind — into the interior space of the Trinity."[2]

In this healing scenario we are faced with experiencing (1) a soothing joy that comes as fear of abandonment dissipates, along with our Pelagian carrying of false crosses, and (2) troubling honesty as we must answer the Triune question of why we have abandoned God to live on our own terms.

It is this healing theological insight of the Triune God, present in suffering Love at Calvary, that is at the center of Mother Teresa's understanding of Ignatian spirituality. Her apprehension is now shared by religious communities known as the Missionaries of Charity. Steeped in the living tradition of the Spiritual Exercises in each of these religious communities above the eucharistic altar hangs a crucifix, and beside it are the words of Jesus, "I thirst" (John 19:28). This, von Balthasar explains, is not a symbol of a separated, dislocated Son from his Father, saying "I thirst." No, it is the Triune God present as Glory at Calvary revealing divine love *thirsting for us!* On the cross it is the Father, Son, and Spirit who speak ineffable words, reaffirming our deepest yearnings for Paradise, pure relating in Love. Though we have criminally sinned against bringing these yearnings, in self-abandoning trust, to the Father through the Spirit groaning to pray in us, Jesus, Father, and Spirit speak Mercy anyway, with internal words: "This day you will be with me in Paradise" (Luke 23:43). There is no dislocated waiting as an isolated individual person. *This day* conveys the Triune truth of loving. It is all so beautiful, so awful, so filled with Love. Can any Calvary ever be experienced again with anti-Christian cynicism, if this small apprehension from von Balthasar's theology grows in heartfelt faith? Jesus, understood as the revelation of the Father's likeness, assures that dark nights will not be without some *sense* of hope that is real. That hope is the Holy Spirit's presence, actively healing and encouraging us as Freedom, though sometimes the Father is experienced as either absent or as calling us to go somewhere we would rather not go.

Calvaries are experienced whenever we feel that God, that Life (John 14:6) is "asking-too-much." Von Balthasar writes:

> This most profound contemplative and dialogic intimacy in which the Father accompanies the Son is the essential presup-

position for the dialogue in the Garden of Olives where the Father as love hides himself and formalizes himself into a *purely* demanding will. It is the presupposition for the way in which all love in the Son is concentrated into the pure, demanded, *asking-too-much* obedience into the all deciding test of strength of divine love in which the Son becomes the "Servant of God" and thus in his exaltation, the Lord. In this, also according to Paul, the justification of all believers and the salvation of the cosmos takes place; in this, according to John, the exalted One on the cross draws all things to himself.[3]

Essentially what I am saying is that von Balthasar's Trinitarian theology, rooted in Ignatian praying, turns against a tendency in Christian spirituality implying that Jesus' appearance in the flesh as God is only a temporary medium, proportional to the weak human condition. Von Balthasar asserts:

Nor is he *a* God, disguised for the time being as a man. Rather, this human personality holding commerce with men is a Person in God; in his mission he not only speaks of the Father, but also represents him, revealing him in every conceivable way, both actively and passively, with power and in weakness, in speech and in silence, veiling and unveiling. And it is this relationship which is the inexhaustible theme, the boundless field, of Christian contemplation.[4]

Of course, the Persons are distinctive and yet One. The *relationships* of Father, Son, and Spirit reveal. It is Jesus, the Son alone, who becomes man, and not the Father or the Spirit. Yet, in seeing Jesus as *the* aesthetic form of beauty we can contemplate the eternal living water flowing in Beauty, relational missions in Trinitarian loving. It is Jesus' human life that "exhibits aspects of his relationship to the Father and to the Spirit."[5]

The basic overview of von Balthasar's understanding of the Trinity begins with Jesus' "descent" into human flesh. In his manner of discourse, what he says, does, and is, Jesus reveals himself to be "self-abasing, humble and obedient love."[6] In explaining Triune Love, von Balthasar simply invites us to contemplate Jesus in Scripture, laying aside prejudices as best we can. He asks us to pray openly, exposing ourselves to the factual healing phenomenon of Jesus Christ. This means, first, believing the biblical facts as historically existent. Through exposing our hearts in an openness that does not prejudge the facts but savors and allows ourselves to inwardly taste them, we are assured by von Balthasar that we will *see* in the Lord's actions, "not only a sublime metaphor of eternal love, but Eternal Love itself."[7] Later, I will address the Ignatian "application of senses" as the ground that informs heartfelt praying in this Triune process of seeing, tasting, and hearing God's love in Jesus. It is, I think, the vital impetus for von Balthasar's years of oceanic writing about the Trinity.

Jesus in Trinitarian contemplation is more than a presence of Eternal Love. According to von Balthasar, Jesus manifests and interprets its very nature, while making Love visible. Jesus' life as Trinitarian Person is not that of a tragic hero or a prophet who suffers for his people. The Son, Jesus, in his self-abasement on earth does not *generally* express God's nature, but the *"particular nature,* the innermost character of the Father who sent him. Jesus is the Father's divine image, his 'Word' like himself a Person: his Son. The Father expresses himself in everything the Son does."[8]

When Jesus' grotesque beauty, in submitting to undergo crucifixion, plunges him into God-forsakenness, von Balthasar explains:

> The Son is giving the ultimate demonstration of how God so loved the world that he gave his only Son: Nothing is feigned here: The Father actually and in all seriousness leaves his Son lying on the ground, in order to go to the stranger, the enemy, man, and to draw him to himself. The Son's passive suffering love becomes at once the upright and the inverted mirror image of the Father's love.[9]

Jesus is thus the appearance of the Father, the Form of creation's forms, of creation's aesthetical structures of beauty (e.g., water and light). Jesus is the central Word of the Father, the light of the Father's love shining *in* darkness. He is not just a prophet who meets revelation and experiences, in the Spirit, the Father's message to preach. Jesus is not a prophetic medium of revelation. He is himself the revelation of God. Von Balthasar asserts that Jesus' form of being is fundamentally different from that of the prophets by pointing to John 3:31–35 and other biblical passages that stress Jesus' *coming* from God. The Baptist and other prophets all had missions, heard God's message within, and delivered that Word to God's people. But Jesus, more than receiving and having a mission, *comes* from above, from God. "By *coming* from the Father he is himself God's form."[10]

In the normative form of Jesus as creature-Creator, in Trinitarian contemplation, von Balthasar finds that we are given a perfect model for our relation to God. In very concrete terms, by contemplating the biblical Jesus "the unapproachable archetype is seen and we come to be absorbed by the understanding that the eternal Triune relationships between Father and Son, in the Spirit, are what makes creation *ad extra* possible."[11] Through Jesus' incarnation, humanity is elevated according to this Trinitarian framework. Jesus elevates us to an accessibility, to an ability to receive healing by relating directly to the Father, in the Spirit. Jesus touches, sees, tastes, hears, and knows the Father in a way which is unique in the intimate inner relationships within the Trinity (John 4:32, 5:19, 6:46, 7:29, 8:26, 8:55).

> As a son of Ignatius Loyola, von Balthasar notes how the author of the Spiritual Exercises employs the senses of the exercitant to draw him/her into the mysteries of the life of Christ. Moreover, in the application of the senses, Ignatius shows how the senses can be integrated into the loving surrender which is prayer. Such use of the senses in prayer should not be considered as lower and inferior form of prayer to be surpassed by a naked mystical intuition of the divine. The senses, healed by grace, can be already mystical.[12]

Now by us seeing, touching, smelling, tasting, hearing an affective knowing of Jesus through contemplation in the Spirit, we have open to us elevating healing grace, the Way, in Jesus, of *sensing* that makes us aware of being in Love beyond all imagining.

The Son is the Spirit-bearer who promises this same Holy Spirit to his followers — through the medium of the senses. Von Balthasar cites Jesus' risen body breathing the Spirit onto/into his followers as he sends them forth to serve in the mission of reconciliation (John 20:21–23). It is a quite sensual scene to openly contemplate, a scene in which Jesus' spiritually risen, embodied senses breathe upon and touch the senses of the apostles. In von Balthasar's understanding of Triune relational loving, Jesus is aware of the wellspring of the Holy Spirit within him (John 7:37, 14:10). It is the Holy Spirit as Person who assumes the leading role in the incarnation, as von Balthasar sees Jesus "allowing himself to be directed."[13] The Holy Spirit is seen as the Freedom of God whose interpersonal relating in the Trinity always presents the Father's will to Jesus, the Son in Love. It is noted by von Balthasar that we do not ever see Jesus in Scripture praying to the Holy Spirit. However, as we contemplate the biblical facts, it becomes clear that Jesus is forever praying in the Spirit (Matt. 4:1). Again, relying on prayer as *sensing,* in a contemplative gazing at Jesus in the mysteries of Scripture, von Balthasar writes, referring to the Person of the Holy Spirit:

> We sense that the innermost being of the Son is "indwelt" in such a way that his own personal will is not interfered with, forced or overpowered; on the contrary this indwelling enables him to realize his own most intimate self. But he does this by being open to the Spirit, by listening and following wherever it blows, and by handing over, entrusting to the Spirit all that he has and is. It is only because there is the Spirit that the Son, as a genuine, limited man, even a weak and failing man, can do his work.[14]

The role of the Holy Spirit is one of bringing balance and calm to what would otherwise be impossible in Jesus' human life. Von Balthasar reminds his readers that Jesus' work ends in failure and death to eyes without faith. But in the Holy Spirit's active loving, Jesus has the ability to "let it be so," to rise from the finality of death, within an entrusting Spirit (Luke 23:46). Because Jesus chooses to abide within the entrusting Spirit he is able to abide within the creaturely truth that human failure praises God. Jesus, instead of going out of his mind with zeal, thinking about what he still has to do, knows the Indwelt Word as "Spirit and Life" (John 6:63). Jesus at Calvary is able, because of the Spirit, to commend himself to the Father (Luke 23:46).

Von Balthasar invites us to contemplate Trinitarian relationships in the Garden of Olives. There "two distinct wills collide 'not my will but thine be done' (Mark 14:36)." The Father's will colliding with his Son's will is evidenced in blood-sweating, wrestling prayer. It is the Spirit as the Freedom of God who stills, calms, and whose mission conveys Love in this inner-Trinitarian conversation. The Son, in Love and in Freedom, allows himself to be directed by not grasping at his divine power (Phil. 2:3–11). Rather, Jesus allows the Spirit to reconcile all sin, all the world, through suffering-servant Love.

Docile to the Spirit he obeys the Father, for the Spirit is the Spirit of the Father: the Spirit brings the Father's will to the Son in a spiritual manner, makes a home for it in him, infuses it into him. But, in obeying, the Son also obeys his own will. This will of his bursts forth from his innermost cove, transporting, and "inspiring" him; it both controls him (as the Father's will) and liberates him (as his own rational and personal will). Through the sovereign freedom of the Person of the Holy Spirit, his will brings him all those things which the Apostle calls the fruits of the Spirit, that inner cataract within the godhead itself: love, joy, peace, patience, kindness, goodness, faithfulness, gentleness, self-control (Gal. 5:22–23).[15]

The diagram[16] that follows is von Balthasar's own effort to depict his theology of Trinitarian relationships, the incarnation, and the binding centrality of Christ as the form-object to be contemplated if we are to see, hear, smell, touch, taste and truly know God's presence in faith.

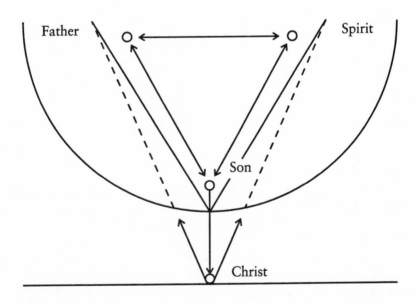

Von Balthasar's overview sees in the Trinity an absolute loving that is "a mutual lack of holding anything back in the three Persons being one-for-another."[17] The inner-Trinitarian life is one, and accordingly this is fraught with experiencing "surprise," since love, even anthropomorphically understood, knows mutual, unconditional self-giving as "gift-in-person."[18] How much more then is Triune mutual loving? Father, Son, and Spirit are personified gifts to each other, and the element of surprise that comes within such love "always transcending the anticipated, is miracle, is experiencing that love is beyond comprehension."[19]

What first seized me while on that Ignatian retreat in Gloucester, Massachusetts, several years ago, can now be somewhat more understood. I should say *who* seized me. The Calvary event was and is dreaded, but now in a fundamental way this dread is less. A small personal apprehension became emblazoned onto my inner-heart, as I opened myself to contemplate the biblical fact of Calvary. Allowing (in the Spirit) my feelings of fear, anger, and confusion to surface, around the colliding inevitability of increased suffering being demanded by Love, the inner dialogic conflict began to be resolved. A heartfelt healing balance was given as a gift that surprised me beyond belief. It was the Holy Spirit as Freedom loving me. The heartfelt fidelity of the Father's will containing Providential Life (amid new dyings) could be accepted and embodied within my own person, carrying a living image of Christ. What had seemed as life asking-too-much, became reconciled by the Spirit as Love. The seemingly cruel abandonment, at the time of crucifixion, was apprehended as a false concept to be winnowed away by the Spirit's healing guidance (Ps. 139:2). Ignatius Loyola wrote about God as Glory alive, not only in the Easter event, but also at the center of Jesus' suffering-servant status. What had been a theological truth, unconnected to my deep affective sensibilities, began to sensibly coalesce within, bringing peace, joy, gentleness, and the knowledge of the Father's faithfulness in Love. Within contemplating Jesus' Calvary, I began to smell a desire to further suffer-with-Jesus so as to glory in Glory. This freedom is Freedom's gift. As always, the struggle continues not to inwardly resist the Spirit's lead, yet this struggle has never been the same, because the foundation shifted within my heart through the Ignatian application of senses in contemplation.

Von Balthasar's chapter on "Triune Life" in *Prayer* concludes with words both sobering and inebriating:

The contemplative, Trinitarian mystery which the Church has gazed upon and which it cherishes in its heart, is not to be belittled by much talking; it brings forth its genuine fruit in those who follow Christ in suffering.[20]

The Trinitarian grounding of von Balthasar's theology of prayer binds the church to contemplate the humanity of Jesus as Son in Sacred Scripture. The practicality and physicality of this avenue of praying always yields more and not less Love. "In the Spirit the person journeys through Christ to the ever greater source of love who is the Father."[21] If individuals or the church are not obedient to this binding, prayer ends up being "daydreaming or conceptual mathematics."[22] Herein lies the vital import for the Ignatian "application of senses."

Von Balthasar knows that "experience" is too easily dichotomized into the sensible and the spiritual. Nondualistic healing prayer is present in what Hugo Rahner describes best:

> The Application of the Senses affects that delicate membrane where body and soul come into most intimate contact and set one another in harmonious motion. The Application of the Senses, therefore, is the great test of whether the technique of meditation has been properly grasped as a whole. According to the instructions given by Ignatius, who was highly experienced in these matters, the Application of the Senses invariably presupposes that the person in question has immersed himself through meditation and contemplation in the truth of salvation proposed to him. Furthermore, as Ignatius and his earliest disciples never tired of emphasizing, there is no such thing as a technique of meditation for its own sake, since genuine meditation is only possible when a person is also prepared to put what he has contemplated into action. *Intelligo ut faciam* — I understand in order that I may act. But the ideas formed in the mind alone must be made to touch the heart before action is possible: and this synthesis of mind and heart takes place precisely in the Application of the Senses, which, because it affects body and soul together, is the most delicate and sensitive form of prayer.[23]

Von Balthasar, very well versed in the Spiritual Exercises, experiences here an avenue in faith that leads to an integrated Christian anthropology. "The application of senses aims at generating a *sentir* of the mysteries of faith: 'a kind of felt knowledge, an affective, intuitive knowledge possessed through the reaction of human feelings to exterior and interior experience.' This *sentir* or heartfelt knowing, indicates the sort of spiritually sensible synthesis which the application seeks to achieve, by focusing the praying person's sensible, affective, volitional and cognitive powers on the Biblical mysteries."[24]

Von Balthasar is interested in the type of prayer that loses itself in its object. "The imagination is the key element in effecting, through the application of senses, a coalescing of all of the powers in human apprehension, into the mystery of God. Faith exercising imagination effects this coalescing which extends from the concreteness of the simple happenings in the Gospels to a point where the Godhead itself becomes concrete by being experienced."[25] It should be recalled that Jesus "the Son is archetype, idea, exemplar of all things outside of God."[26] And because he is the absolute self-expression of God as such, Jesus is both Power and Beauty in the created order, drawing all things to himself, ordering beauty through Love. "Since the sensory environment is determined and given meaning through the central event of Christ, the very environment becomes a theatre or radiant monstrance of God's real presence."[27] Von Balthasar's framework of Trinitarian relationships takes us into a theological aesthetic that heals our senses. It takes us to see Beauty, Jesus, in the grotesque ugliness of innocent suffering, hanging on a cross.

Von Balthasar's Trinitarian grounding for healing prayer invites us to contemplate and thus sensually appropriate the depths of God's desire to be Love-for-us and Love-with-us, remaining with us even when we reject(ed) him. The paradox of ugliness and Beauty being one, in the Calvary event, "reveals the depths to which God will go to be consistent with himself. On the cross God reveals himself as pure, unbounded Love."[28] Instead of revealing himself as pure unbounded power, or pure unbounded beauty, Jesus as the Son reveals the Father in the Spirit of suffering Pure Love. Powerlessness and power, ugliness and beauty paradoxically are synthesized in and by a greater harmony that is *the Word,* made flesh in Jesus, Love. Hearing this music, this Inner Word, as we pray through our own calvaries, inevitably soothes the human heart and brings us to experience new life.

It is fitting to end this segment with a famous quote from Augustine's *Confessions* that seems to illustrate so much of what has been said:

What is it that I love when I love my God? It is a certain light that I love and melody, and fragrance, and embrace that I love when I love my God — a light, melody, fragrance, food, embrace of the God within, where, for my soul, that shines which space does not contain; that sounds which time does not sweep away; that is fragrant which the breeze does not dispel; and that tastes sweet which no satiety disparts — this is what I love when I love my God.[29]

Chapter Nine

IGNATIAN SPIRITUAL DIRECTION AND INNER DYNAMICS OF THE HEART

Images speak, think, and evoke heartfelt interior movements within us, within our souls. And so my model for spiritual direction, and the inner dynamics of the heart, can best be expressed through envisioning the image of a midwife assisting in the birth of new life.

Daily, we inwardly carry the death and the new life of Christ (2 Cor. 4:10–11) groaning within us, along with all creation (Rom. 8:16–25). The analogy of spiritual direction as "midwifing" emphasizes several critical aspects of this art. It is an image that conveys the primacy of all other goals, namely, to companion the directee in giving birth, through a relationship with Christ Jesus, the source of all new life. The midwife's focus requires a putting aside of self-concerns in an active passivity, an active, prayerful waiting. He or she assists in a process that receives its relational energy from God's active desiring as "Energy, Holy Spirit."[1] It was and is God's initiative and desire to create us, and to re-create us in baptism, making all of us new, as children (Rom. 6:1–4, 8:14–17). The image of the director as midwife evokes a "suffering-with" knowledge that anticipates future consolation for the directee which always follows the pain of human spiritual growth. The imaginative truth of "midwifery" as a working model speaks of our co-laboring being both active and passive. God induces the laboring through foundational loving, this being experienced as very alive in faith through the heartfelt comings and goings of God's presence. The directee carries new life and is forever called to co-labor within the familial Trinity by noticing, attending to, and enhancing this new life, in the service of self-love and love of neighbor (Mark 12:30–31). The director co-labors by a self-emptying assistance in the unfolding relationship between the directee and God. Analogously the midwife coaches, converses with to encourage, counsels, gets his or her hands messy in helping throughout, cleans up afterbirth, and sometimes intervenes by adjusting the baby in the womb, easing the birthing process. Yet, the director's ministry as midwife remains primarily an active passivity, accompanying in silent hopefulness a relational process initiated and promoted by God in the heart of the directee (2 Thess. 1:11). Finally, the director in midwifery has the privilege of presenting what already is, engendering awe as the directee sees mirrored back the shameless, pure love of God in the gift of a new life forever arriving.

The overall worldview in this ministerial posture portrays the universe as the womb of God, a womb that exists because of, and through, the nourishing Heart of Jesus. It is both ordinary and concrete, as well as extraordinary and cosmic imaginative truth. Midwifery models spiritual direction well in that it builds upon the historical tradition of the director as a "doctor of souls," while avoiding the overintrusive, fix-it associations often related with medical care in our time. Midwifery has been a prevailing phenomenon throughout history, and it poignantly reflects my own experience in the ministry of spiritual direction. Reportedly, "midwives still assist in eighty percent of childbirths worldwide."[2]

Though the image of midwifery seems very adequate in depicting a working model, all analogies fall short of expressing the multilayered dimensions of mystery at work in the awe-inspiring dynamics of the human heart. In his enormously rich book *Soul Friend,* Kenneth Leech quotes Max Thurian to define the art of spiritual direction:

> Spiritual direction, or the cure of souls, is a seeking after the leading of the Holy Spirit in a given psychological and spiritual situation. Here the stress is on *seeking*, and the seeking is mutual. The director, and the person being directed, are both seekers: they are both parts of a spiritual direction, a current of spirituality, a divine-human process of relationship. Spirituality and spiritual life are not religious departments, walled off areas of life. Rather the spiritual life is the life of the whole person directed toward God.[3]

In a generic way this describes the goal of spiritual direction in different words: seeking, finding and deepening our relationship with Christ's Spirit.

Understanding the basic inner dynamics of the human heart is, of course, critical for the person called to this ministry. Martin Thornton, in the Anglican tradition, sees spiritual direction as the primary concern of the Christian priest or minister. Essential to efficacious laboring in the church is personal prayer and the study of ascetical theology. Wholeheartedly agreeing with Thornton, I too want to stress the centrality of acquiring expertise in a life of prayer. Thornton writes:

> I suspect that intelligent modern Christians are getting suspicious of clergy who are forever engaged in something other than prayer, learning and such like professional occupations. …It is because a priest has time for prayer, study and reflection that his guidance of those in the hurly burly is likely to be worth having.[4]

Because Christian spirituality is not a walled-off compartment to take care of as a duty in a person's everyday checklist of works to do, "prayer time" must be recognized as a time of especially focused inner relating. It is a quality time of conversing in friendship with God's Spirit (John 15:14). Prayer acts like a magnifying lens and like an amplifier. Prayer enlarges the echoes of God's Word, affectively active within us. It magnifies, and thus reveals, ongoing affective movements in the human heart.

A biblically accurate understanding names prayer as an openness to what Karl Rahner, as a companion of Ignatius, calls "everyday mysticism," wherein the human heart "feels after and finds God" (Acts 17:27) in ordinary living. The inner dynamics of the "heart" for Rahner are best understood through "the guiding threads of affective intentionality, affective connaturality, and habit as virtue. Affective consciousness (heart) is not reducible to cognitive, volitional consciousness"[5] nor is it mere inner moods or surface feelings. Rather, affective consciousness presents us with and is our very ground of being. Indeed, beneath Freud's pleasure-pain principles operative in all of us lie heart-feelings that call us to Christ's friendship and eternal life (John 15:8–17).

Ignatius of Loyola referred to heart-feelings or deep interior affective movements (spirits) with the Spanish word *sentir*. With its full meaning *sentir* connotes heartfelt impulses that ground being itself, affective movements through which emotions, will, and intellect are all coalescing in human experience. Awareness of these interior affective movements, which are always addressing us (Rom. 8:26–

27), makes possible an ongoing heart-to-Heart conversation with Jesus, the living Word and Heart of the world (John 1:1–5), the ground of all being (Rev. 1:17–18). Listening for and entering into this conversing brings about everyday mysticism.

Whereas "classical mysticism" refers to prayer as infused contemplation, historically reserved for unusually gifted members of the faith community, "everyday mysticism" refers to ordinary believers who regularly experience a realization of God's presence with us and taste our transforming participation in Christ's life.

> Characteristic to note in the everyday mystic's life experience include: (1) a special awareness or conviction that she or he is being guided by the God-life, the Christ-life, (2) an element of passivity or receptivity regarding God's presence, (3) a qualitatively special knowledge and loving wisdom and, (4) a tasting of grace as a unifying force profoundly uniting us in love with God, neighbor, and the Christ-self.[6]

How does this prayerful heart-to-Heart conversation work? For Ignatius, affective consciousness carries the dynamic capacity of affective imagining that is ever present, and by learning to exercise this in-built capacity for heartfelt knowing the believer can savor and increasingly enjoy the eschatological promises of Jesus Christ (John 14:1–21).

By spiritually exercising our inner attention, through a personal heartfelt conversation with Jesus in the Scriptures, affective "imagination"[7] within us experiences connective feelings being evoked in relationship with the divine Word. This discourse is typified by spiritual writers as either kataphatic (with images) or apophatic (without images). But whether the believer's heart experiences non-visual clouds of unknowing (see William Johnston, *The Mysticism of the Cloud of Unknowing* [New York: Harper & Row, 1967]) or active dialoguing with visualized images, the undergirding affective imaginative consciousness is being engaged through heart-feelings in an interpersonal, spiritually dynamic conversation with Christ, as indwelling Spirit.

One scholar more technically describes the process:

> The intellect and will become affective in two ways: the soul as *anima corporis* sinks into its roots in instinct and embodiment, and as spirit it ascends beyond the complexity of discursive rea-

son and deliberative volition in interpersonal relations where connaturality based on virtue leads to a simplification, healing, elevation and improvement of our operations of knowing and loving. This second way is not feeling in a "lower" sentimental sense but experience as felt harmony and resonance in one's spiritual being.[8]

Praying may take the believer to feel God's absence or God's presence. Either way affective conscious imagining gives us pre-conceptual heart-feelings of basic consolation or desolation. These heart-feelings need to be tasted and communicated interpersonally with God for healing love to deepen and be realized. Being in touch with and living out of preconceptual affective consciousness is essential to spiritual growth because "the function of feeling is to bind together. It connects what knowledge divides; it binds me to things, to beings, to being. The whole movement of objectification tends to set a world over against me, feeling unites the intentionality that throws me out of myself, to the affection through which I feel myself existing."[9]

If we really knew who it was who is addressing us affectively and offering us a conversation in the wellsprings of our heart's desiring (John 4:10) we would drink in unreservedly, moved by our infinitely thirsty need to be satiated by Love (1 John 4:1-3).

A psychological phenomenology of heartfelt "desiring" seems to provide the best avenue for prayerful reflection on human experience in spiritual direction. It is this avenue, beautifully expanded upon by Ann and Barry Ulanov in their book *Primary Speech,* that contains specific details of my working model. In a nutshell, their chapter entitled "Prayer and Desire" articulates the interplay of psychological and spiritual movements at work in religious experiences. It is pertinent to make clear that Webster's Dictionary defines a desire as "an inclination toward some object accompanied by a positive affect." Ignatius Loyola's operative understanding is quite similar. The inclination at prayer is toward relating interpersonally with God, the objective reality outside ourselves is God who is love (1 John 4:16). When interiorly connected with God this inclination always carries some heartfelt consolation.

Simply, I want to list a few quotations from the Ulanovs which convey the framework and value of approaching spiritual direction through a psychological phenomenology of "desiring":

All prayer begins with desire.... At its best, desire in prayer is what Augustine calls an affectionate reaching out to God.[10]

Augustine put it succinctly in his observation that prayer is the construction of our desires.[11]

Choice presents itself early on in prayer. We discover levels to our desire. We want lesser things; we want greater things . . . to languish in the lesser pleasures and to refuse the greater that God offers . . . that is sin.[12]

Prayer enlarges our desire until it receives God's desire for us. In prayer we grow big enough to house God's desire in us which is the Holy Spirit.[13]

The minister as spiritual director works knowing that one aspect of the heart's activity, such as the emotions, thinking, or willing, can be overemphasized. By focusing on the phenomena of desiring, a harmonious coalescing of the heart's activities can be seen occurring in the directee's relationship with the Holy Spirit. And attending to this relationship is really the only reason for spiritual direction.

Building upon the basic inner dynamics of the human heart, Ignatius Loyola transcribed experiential insights that accurately guide and illuminate our prayerful desiring and seeking, our midwifery in spiritual direction. These transcriptions (see Appendix I, "Guidelines for the Discernment of Spirits") blend a phenomenology of our greatest desires with a theological anthropology of inner affective movements (spirits). This results in a profoundly personal call to holiness. This is an experiential theology of interior conversation promising appropriations of Christ's healing grace.

It bears repeating that spiritual consolation as a general fundamental category for interior affective movements has as many names as there are experiences of consolation in life. Some synonyms and/or derivatives for consolation are heartfelt gentleness, peace, calm, relief, soothing joy, and any felt increase in faith, hope, or love. Sadness that surfaces and then dissipates (often through tears) is also spiritual consolation (Sp. Ex. #318–19).

Ignatian theological anthropology conveys the experienced truth of spiritual desolation as a second encompassing category, describing our heartfelt, inner movements. Examples of affective stirrings in this category include melancholy, agitation, anxiety, and any diminishment of faith, hope, or love, or the increasing weight of sadness

(Sp. Ex. #317). These experiential movements never point to the Holy Spirit's urgings or inner-felt word. In desolation, the enemy of human nature guides, lures, and counsels the heart (Sp. Ex. #6).

Harvey Egan's work entitled *The Ignatian Mystical Horizon* gives an unparalleled description of the heartfelt interplay of desire and consoling and desolate affective movements within the believer who is engaged in the Spiritual Exercises.

> The exercitant progresses during the Exercises if he receives the "what I want and desire" graces of each particular meditation. He must experience, during his meditations on the great truths of salvation history, various interior movements which Ignatius calls consolation (Sp. Ex. #316). These consolations in turn, must become an actual state of soul....
>
> Ignatius, moreover, clearly expects more during the Exercises than consolation. He knows that the generous exercitant will experience consolations, desolations and be moved by various spirits (Sp. Ex. #6).
>
> It should be mentioned that desolations have many valuable lessons to teach. Desolation can awaken a lax conscience (Sp. Ex. #314), bring a person's sloth and tepidity to light (Sp. Ex. #322), test and teach the person that consolations are strictly God's gifts (Sp. Ex. #322). And yet, Ignatius always has the believer fight this experienced state of the soul (Sp. Ex. #319), understanding that the pain of growth, as in giving birth, is always followed by a greater joy. The special significance of consolations and desolations resides in the existential truth that they manifest our hidden affections which either help or hinder his/her basic anthropocentric dynamism to come to ourselves and surrender to the loving Mystery of God in Jesus Christ (Col. 3:1–4). In other words, spiritual consolations and desolations are the positive and negative echoes of a person's own being, to the deepest demands of the true, hidden self. The believer's consolations and desolations, peace and disharmony are the profound signs of self-surrender or self-refusal to the deepest anthropocentric drawings, abiding and active in the human heart.
>
> In Ignatian discernment, when a person prays over the life, death, and resurrection of Jesus Christ, his or her deepest nature is evoked and enlightened. Consolations and desolations

are experienced while praying with Christ in Sacred Scripture, and they are a measure of the soundness or sickness of the person's human nature. Thus, desolation can be understood as the inner repugnance which flows from a person's disorientation and resistance to the deep demands of becoming more fully human, more full of love. Desolation highlights the praying person's hidden resistance to full self-identity, as well as those areas in the person's being which prevent authentic human growth. Desolation exposes a person's affective disorder and allows him/her to work out inordinate attachments, to allow healing in much the same way that a person works out a cramp in a muscle. The generosity and progress the exercitant makes in knowing, loving and serving Christ indirectly deepens and strengthens his own human nature.[14]

Spiritual consolations will always be experienced in the person's heart as the more natural, more fitting, deeper, truer experience. Desolations will be experienced as something running counter to a person's authentic inner core. It is somehow an unnatural experience, because our spiritual kinship within God's womb always resonates in the depths of our being. Thomas Aquinas names this experience of resonance as a form of "connaturality."

> The operative questions for the spiritual director and directee are: what has been happening in our hearts, how have we experienced the Lord's presence laboring in love, what has the Holy Spirit been asking us, and where do we feel Christ's Spirit leading us? Again, interior feelings, urges and movements are the "spirits" that must be sifted out, discerned so we can recognize Christ's Spirit calling to us in the intimate core of our being.[15]

Admittedly painting with extremely broad strokes, I wish to offer a few significant connections between insights from several major authors and the process of Ignatian discernment. James Fowler and Robert Kegan, contemporary researchers in the areas of developmental psychology and spiritual maturation, highly value the intentional providing of "holding environments — safe places in which persons can do the frightening work of deconstruction and reconstruction."[16] Spiritual direction explicitly is this sort of relationship. It attempts to guard against the transferences of the minister's own hopes and values for the sake of "the psychological and philosophical development of the truth, ... truth being an activity of relating or balance."[17] Ignatian spiritual direction fosters the concrete and cosmic world-view that spiritual relating brings us to see reality itself as the womb of God, holding us in natural, nurturing Love, amid terrors and fears that need not be debilitating to the human spirit. Through consciously tasting the love of God in a sustained prayerful "holding environment," an ongoing healing of shame and fear can occur. Alice Miller writes convincingly about the negative effects in early childhood of a mother's gaze inducing shame, a shame that causes harmful compulsions rooted in the need to feel worthy and good. Miller writes about a man's need for healing:

> Social pressures take on unnecessary proportions because his psyche has been formed and anchored in his earliest affective experience ... His problems cannot be solved with words, but only through experience, ... not merely by corrective experience as an adult but, above all, through a reliving of his early fear of his beloved mother's contempt and his subsequent feelings of indignation and sadness.[18]

Ignatian prayer and discernment promote the healing experience that Miller calls for and restores us to the truth affectively imagined by God in our baptism. In real prayer, primal fears and sadnesses are gradually relived in the light of a gaze that delights in us (Matt. 3:16–17), relieving toxic shame, restoring us to original innocence. Shame and its associated meanings inevitably surface in spiritual direction when the structure of one's desiring in prayer is attended to with reverence. The application of Ignatian discernment asks the essential question of what inner affective movements accompany experiences of shame. Differentiation can then occur and a pastoral diagnostic wisdom can dawn. The director, as doctor of the soul, assists the directee in distinguishing between shame that needs to surface and be let go of and shame that is meant to be accepted as a grace. One type of shame is to be unlearned as we more freely embrace the sheer goodness and beauty of our humanity. Another type of shame is a special invitation to share intimately the humiliation Jesus experienced as he was insulted and persecuted for justice' sake (Luke 6:22–23; James 1:2–4, 4:1–3). Some shame stems from a culture shackled by the demon of consumerism. This kind of shame attaches itself to an individual's desiring and speaks of the false need to indulge in commodities in the hope of acquiring personal fulfillment and satisfactions. Identifying the *attached affections* (consolations or desolations) in discerning a person's shame breeds ascetical wisdom and promotes true Christian growth, becoming more like Christ (Gal. 2:19–20).

A similar connection can be made between Ernest Becker's major insights in his classic *The Denial of Death*. As Becker summed up his reflections, he wrote:

> I think that taking life seriously means something such as this: that whatever man does on this planet has to be done in the lived truth of the terror of creation, of the grotesque, of the rumble of panic underneath everything.... Otherwise, it is false.[19]

He saw that much of science and psychology dehumanized us by trying to take away the terror of our incarnational fragility. Ignatian anthropology and the Guidelines for Discernment support Becker's thesis. Spiritual consolations go against what Becker rightly sees as a bourgeois calming of terror and invites the existential realities to surface (see Sp. Ex. #45–72, meditations on temptation, sin, and hell). Spiritual consolations always strengthen a person's ability to be more deeply accepting and loving in the face of real terrors in the night. Death itself is a mere creature for Ignatius, not carrying the final word. Yet, fear of death is part of daily authentic praying as everyday mystics take up their crosses, follow, and lose themselves in Jesus' risen presence so as to find themselves (Matt. 16:21–27). Certain creaturely fears are not to be removed by the science or art of spiritual direction. Desolation will increase the more religion is used as an opiate, anesthetizing us from reality. A differentiation of heartfelt affective movements (through applying Ignatius Loyola's guidelines for discernment) will reveal if a directee is being strengthened, growing positively in the Holy Spirit's awe-inspiring gift of "fear of the Lord," or if the fears are from the evil spirit, the enemy of human nature. Fears of this latter type, which are debilitating, can be worked out and gradually healed, as mentioned previously, much like a cramped muscle is relieved, by spiritually massaging it. Becker's diagnosis of our need "to project problems onto a god-figure, to be healed by an all-embracing and all-justifying beyond,"[20] resonates with Ignatian advice in the *Spiritual Exercises*. Such an exercise is part of spiritual healing. Ignatius invites projected fears to meet the reality of God's Love (1 John 4:16) as part of the true inner dynamic of our being conscious, of relating to God's presence (Luke 1:46–55, Rom. 8:26–27). Prayer in the Spiritual Exercises like all prayer begins wherever we find ourselves to be and heals us gradually of fears, most especially the fear of death. Ignatian anthropology knows developmentally speaking that "we come to God at first through the way we need God to be, and that only slowly and with much experience in prayer can we allow God to come to us."[21] Inner personal illusions betraying a lack of inner freedom to relate to reality as it is will be accompanied by an interior affective desolation. Inner unfreedoms or experiential desolations in faith become resolved by a sustained heartfelt honesty in conversation with God, much like we find depicted in the affective expressions of the Psalms. Affective projections are important.

> We must bring all of our pictures of God right into our prayers as the centerpiece of our offerings and as something we present to and talk over with God. Those images and names that entrap us will be loosened. Those that block conversation will be winnowed out. Those that push to center stage, eclipsing both ourselves and the God we address, will be broken.[22]

And those projections that mirror Christ's abiding Heart, the ground of all reality (John 1:1–5, 1 Cor. 13:12–13), will be a source of grace, producing healing effects.

The chart on the following page lists general relational effects which signify healing. These relational effects mean that interior affective phenomena, presenting the indwelling Word, have been noticed, acknowledged, and responded to in faith.

Chapters 1, 2, 3, and 4 consisted of retrospective personal stories that illuminate experiences of partially appropriating Christ's healing grace. Two chapters are derived from participants who engaged in prayerful conversation in the Spiritual Exercises through the context of the "at-home" twenty-four week format. The other two chapters reflect upon the experience from within the "retreat house," thirty-day format. Evidence of the participants' everyday mysticism in which they each realize Christ's story as their own, and the resultant healing effects, can instruct, inform, and encourage those who labor in the art of Ignatian spiritual direction. In each story the "Guidelines for the Discernment of Spirits" (see Appendix I) can be employed for pastoral diagnosis.

By listening to the words of Gerald May an appreciation for

Relational Effects That Signify Healing

Interior Effects GALATIANS 5:22–23 EPHESIANS 3:16–19	*External Behavioral Effects* MATTHEW 5:1–12 MATTHEW 25:31–46
Increased Love	• Decreased Violence Toward Self and Others • Increased Affirmation Toward Self and Others
Increased Joy	• Decreased Cynicism in Conversation and Humor • Increased Rejoicing, Mourning, and Celebrating
Increased Peace	• Decreased Avoidance of Engaging in Conflicts • Increased Mediation in Conflicts

Increased Patience	• Decreased Overextension in Use of Time
	   and Purchasing Material Goods
	• Increased Simplification in Using Time
	   and Purchasing Material Goods

Increased Kindness	• Decreased Omission of Comforting the Poor,
	   Afflicted, and Marginalized
	• Increased Service in Comforting the Poor,
	   Afflicted, and Marginalized

Increased Goodness	• Decreased Self-Concern in Prayer • Increased Intercession for Others in Prayer
Increased Trustfulness	• Decreased Withdrawal from Relationships • Increased Commitment in Relationships
Increased Gentleness	• Decreased Acting Out in Anger • Increased Acts of Mercy
Increased Self-Control	• Decreased Compulsions • Increased Free Choices
Increased Hope	• Decreased Recriminations • Increased Endurance in Suffering Injustice

---

the ongoing need to discern the meaning of lively pain is brought into focus.

To live as a child of God is to live with love, hope, and growth, but it is also to live with longing, with aching for a fullness of love that is never quite within our grasp. Our fundamental disease, then, is at once a precise neurological phenomenon and a most precious gift from God. It is not a sign of something wrong, but of something more profoundly right than we could ever dream of.[23]

And so our aches need to be discerned. Is this or that ache accompanied by heartfelt consolation or desolation? Is this or that ache signifying a sickness to be healed, a disorder in the affections (Matt. 9:10–13), or is it an ache signifying holiness and wholeness? Some aches are God-like passions to rest in with growing trust, as we experience the Holy Spirit's power amid powerlessness (2 Cor. 12:10). To follow Christ in authentic discipleship amid spiritual direction requires a vigilant relearning of these differentiations. In spiritual direction as midwifing we always await a further coming of God's glory (Eph. 3:16–19) and testify with St. Paul that the whole creation is groaning with desires and eager longings. From the beginning up to the present day, creation has been groaning in one great act of giving birth. Ignatian spiritual direction as "midwifery" multiplies our tasting of the first-fruits of the Holy Spirit (Gal. 5:22–26). This relational art yields interpenetrating awe, wonder, and gratitude, relying upon God's abiding desire to complete our joy (John 15:11–12), always drawing us into the mystery of becoming a new creation (2 Cor. 5:17).

Appendix 1

GUIDELINES FOR THE DISCERNMENT OF SPIRITS

Preliminary Note:
On the Use of "Spirits," Good and Evil
by David L. Fleming, S.J.

"Discernment of spirits" is a venerable phrase of the Christian spiritual tradition. From the action of good or evil spirits upon one result "movements of one's heart or spirit," "motions affecting one's interior life," "a certain impetus in one's life," "a feeling for or against some course of action," and so on. The descriptive words "good" and "evil" as applied to "spirits" are used to designate primarily the source or cause of the movement or feeling as a good or an evil spirit. What we experience, however, is that good spirits lead a person in a good direction toward a good goal. Evil spirits make use of evil directions, and even sometimes of what are at first good directions, to accomplish an evil end.

Although the importance of these movements comes in the direction which they give to our lives, we are necessarily concerned about recognizing their good or evil source, especially in view of the possible deception of an apparently good direction. In light of modern psychology, we have some indications of the great complexity of human motivations. Added to this complexity of human motivation, we Christians live in a faith-world which acknowledges the unfathomable power of evil personified in Satan and the damned of hell and the even more mysterious power of good focused in God and in the communion of saints. And so when we attempt to say something not only about the direction of these spirits but also about what the sources of these good and evil spirits or motions are, we can still find helpful a scheme adapted and expanded from the traditional Ignatian division (Sp. Ex. #32):

Good spirits and evil spirits come from
  1. *within our very selves, or*
  2. *outside of us, from*
     1. *our fellow men, or*
     2. *power more than human.*

Although as redeemed sinners we can confess that both good and evil motions emanate from within us, we still stand amazed at both the good and the evil which comes forth from the heart of us human beings. Like St. Paul in his seventh chapter of the Letter to the Romans, we suffer from the divisions we feel within our very selves. In fact, we commonly feel more comfortable to be able to blame evil on someone or something outside of ourselves. Even the first sin of man and woman is pictured in such a way in the third chapter of Genesis when Adam attempts to shift the blame to Eve, and Eve looks to the serpent. Yet without in any way lessening our own potential human malice, we have experientially as well as scripturally the evidence of a power of evil that is bigger than any one person or group of people. Just as our fellowmen can influence our choices and action toward wrong, so too the "more than human" power of evil is destructive and deadly in its enticements and enslavements. While our fellowmen can also be an influence for good, we know similarly from experience and from Scripture another power of good, which comes from God Himself directly intervening in our lives as well as the continuing intercession of the saints who have gone before us.

In the following guidelines for discerning spirits, an attempt is made to give helps to develop an ability to recognize ever earlier the direction of certain movements or feelings in our lives, and so to be able to follow or reject them almost in their very sources.

PART I.
Guidelines Suitable Especially for the First Week*

The statements below are an attempt to present certain norms which might be helpful in understanding different interior movements which happen in the "heart" of man and woman. By the grace of God, we are meant to recognize those that are good so that we might let them give direction to our lives and those that are bad so that we might reject them or turn aside from them.

The norms in this first section are more appropriate to the kind of spiritual experiences associated with the First Week of the Exercises.

A. Two Statements of General Application

1. When we are caught up in a life of sin or perhaps even if we [314] are closed off from God in only one area of our life, the evil spirit is ordinarily accustomed to propose a slothful complacency or a future of ever greater pleasures still to be grasped. He fills our imagination with all kinds of sensual delights so that there is no will or desire to change the evil directions of our life.

The good spirit uses just the opposite method with us. He will try to make us see the absurdity of the direction our life has taken. Little by little an uneasiness described sometimes as the "sting" of conscience comes about and a feeling of remorse sets in.

2. When we are intent upon living a good life and seeking to pur- [315] sue the lead of God in our life, the tactics of the spirits are just the opposite of those described above.

The evil spirit proposes to us all the problems and difficulties in living a good life. The evil spirit attempts to rouse a false sadness for things which will be missed, to bring about anxiety about persevering when we are so weak, to suggest innumerable roadblocks in walking the way of the Lord. And so the evil spirit tries discouragement and deception to deter us from growing in the Christ-life.

The good spirit, however, strengthens and encourages, consoles and inspires, establishes a peace and sometimes moves to a firm resolve. To lead a good life gives delight and joy, and no obstacle seems

---

*The selections that follow are taken from David L. Fleming, S.J., *The Spiritual Exercises of Saint Ignatius of Loyola: A Literal Translation and a Contemporary Reading*, reprinted with permission of the Institute of Jesuit Sources, St. Louis, Mo.

to be so formidable that it cannot be faced and overcome. The good
spirit thereby continues an upright person's progress in the Lord.

B. Particular Statements Referring Especially to Persons Intent upon Changing Their Lives and Doing Good

First of all, two terms should be defined:

[316]   3. *Spiritual consolation.* This term describes our interior life:

    a. when we find ourselves so on fire with the love of God
that neither anything nor anyone presents itself in com-
petition with a total gift of self to God in love. Rather
we begin to see everything and everyone in the context of
God, their Creator and Lord;

    b. when we are saddened, even to the point of tears, for our
infidelity to God but at the same time thankful to know
God as Savior. Such consolation often comes in a deep
realization of ourselves as sinners before a God who loves
us, or in the face of Christ's Passion when we see that
Jesus loves his Father and his fellowmen so much, or for
any other reason which leads us to praise and thank and
serve God all the better;

    c. when we find our life of faith, hope, and love so strength-
ened and emboldened that the joy of serving God is
foremost in our life. More simply said, consolation can
be found in any increase of our faith, our hope, and
our love. A deep-down peace comes in just "being in my
Father's house."

[317]   4. *Spiritual desolation.* This term describes our interior life:

    a. when we find ourselves enmeshed in a certain turmoil
of spirit or feel ourselves weighted down by a heavy
darkness or weight;

    b. when we experience a lack of faith or hope or love in the
very distaste for prayer or for any spiritual activity and
we know a certain restlessness in our carrying on in the
service of God;

    c. when we experience just the opposite effect of what has
been described as spiritual consolation. For we will notice

that the thoughts of rebelliousness, despair, or selfishness which arise at the time of desolation are in absolute contrast with the thoughts of the praise and service of God which flow during the time of consolation.

Four guidelines dealing with spiritual desolation now follow:

5. When we find ourselves weighed down by a certain desolation, [318] we should not try to change a previous decision or to come to a new decision. The reason is that in desolation the evil spirit is making an attempt to obstruct the good direction of our life or to change it, and so we would be thwarted from the gentle lead of God and what is more conducive to our own salvation. As a result, at a time of desolation, we hold fast to the decision which guided us during the time before the desolation came on us.

6. Although we should not try to make new decisions at a time [319] of desolation, we should not just sit back and do nothing. We are meant to fight off whatever is making us less than we should be. And so we might try to intensify our prayer, we might take on some penance, or we might make a closer examination of ourselves and our life of faith.

7. Oftentimes in desolation we feel that God has left us to fend for [320] ourselves. By faith we know that he is always with us in the strength and power of his grace, but at the time of apparent abandonment we are little aware of his care and concern. We experience neither the support nor the sweetness of his love, and our own response lacks fervor and intensity. It is as if we are living a skeletal life of the bare bones of faith.

8. The important attitude to nourish at a time of desolation is [321] patience. Patience can mitigate the frustration, dryness, or emptiness of the desolation period and so allow us to live through it a little less painfully. We should try to recall that everything has its time, and consolation has been ours in the past and will be God's gift in the future. Patience should mark even the efforts we undertake to work against the desolation which afflicts us.

9. Three important reasons why we suffer desolation are: [322]

1. it is our own fault because we have not lived our life of faith with any effort. We have become tepid and slothful and our very shallowness in the spiritual life has brought about the experience of desolation;

2. it is a trial period allowed by God. We find ourselves tested as to whether we love God or just love his gifts, whether we continue to follow his call in darkness and dryness as well as in light and consolation;

3. it is a time when God lets us experience our own poverty and need. We see more clearly that the free gift of consolation is not something we can control, buy, or make our own.

Next follow two guidelines with spiritual consolation:

[323] 10. When we are enjoying a consolation period, we should use foresight and savor the strengths of such a period against the time we may no longer find ourselves in consolation.

[324] 11. A time of consolation should provide the opportunity for a growth in true humility. We can acknowledge with gratitude the gifts we have received and recognize the full gratuity of God's favor. It may be well to take stock how poorly we fare when such consolation is withdrawn.

On the other hand, if we are afflicted by desolation, we should take some consolation in knowing that God's grace is always sufficient to follow the way of the Lord.

Through three images we can understand better the ways in which the evil spirit works.

[325] 12. The evil spirit often behaves like a spoiled child. If a person is firm with such a child, the child gives up his petulant ways. But if a person shows indulgence or weakness in any way, the child is merciless in getting his own way by stomping his feet or by false displays of affection. So our tactics must include firmness in dealing with the evil spirit in our lives.

[326] 13. The evil spirit's behavior can also be compared to a false lover. The false lover uses other people for his own selfish ends, and so he uses people like objects at his disposal or as his playthings for entertainment and good times. He usually suggests that the so-called intimacy of the relationship be keep secret because he is afraid that his duplicity will become known. So the evil spirit often acts in order to keep his own suggestions and temptations secret, and our tactics must be to bring out into the light of day such suggestions and temptations to our confessor or director or superior.

[327] 14. The evil spirit can also work like a shrewd army commander who carefully maps out the tactics of attack at weak points of

the defense. He knows that weakness if found in two ways: (a) the weakness is fragility or unpreparedness, and (b) the weakness of complacent strength which is pride. The evil spirit's attacks come against us at both of these points of weakness. The first kind of weakness is less serious in that we more readily acknowledge our need and cry out for help to the Lord. The second kind is far more serious and more devastating in its effect upon us so that it is a more favored tactic of the evil spirit.

PART II.
Guidelines Suitable Especially for the Second Week

The following statements are also meant to be helpful in under-   [328]
standing the interior movements which are a part of our spiritual lives. These guidelines are more subtle than the norms described in Part I because commonly in the progress of a good person's life the direction of all movements appears to be toward God and the proper development of one's spiritual life. These norms are especially helpful when a person experiences certain movements that commonly occur to persons engaged in the Second Week of the Exercises or thereafter.

A. A Statement of General Applications

1. When we are trying to follow the call of the Lord in our life, we   [329]
will find that the good spirit tends to give support, encouragements, and oftentimes even a certain delight in all our endeavors.

The evil spirit generally acts to bring about the opposite reaction. The evil spirit will subtly arouse a dissatisfaction with our own efforts, will raise up doubts and anxieties about God's love or our own response, or sting the conscience with thoughts of pride in our attempt to lead a good life.

B. Particular Statements about Consolation

First, consolation is described in terms of its sources.

2. God alone can bring about consolation without any concomi-   [330]
tant causes. We know the experience of having certain thoughts, achievements, or events which bring about a feeling of great consolation in our lives. We also know the effect of another person or

persons whose very presence or conversation can give us joy. But we can more readily attribute our consolation directly to the touch of God when there is no thought, no event, no person — in general, no object of any sort — which seems to be the source of such a movement. The directness of sense words, such as "a touch" or "a taste," seems to point more accurately the way to describe this special action of God in our lives. The effect of such a taste or touch, which may bring along delight or joy, is what we can more readily grasp and speak about. But in these cases, we should be aware that God himself is truly said to be the direct source of all our consolation.

[331]   3. When there is a reason for consolation, whether it be from certain thoughts or achievements or events, or even more so from certain people who have an effect upon us, then either the good spirit or the evil spirit can be involved. On the other hand, the good spirit brings about such consolation in order to strengthen and to speed the progress of our life in Christ. The evil spirit, on the other hand, arouses good feelings so that we are drawn to focus our attention on wrong things, or to pursue a more selfish motivation, or to find our own will before all else. Quietly and slowly the change is brought about until the evil direction becomes clear.

Ways of working with spurious consolation are:

[332]   4. For a person striving to lead a good life, the evil spirit ordinarily begins like an angel of light. For example, we find ourselves inspired by pious thoughts or holy desires, and then after some time we are caught up in the pride of our own intellect and in the selfishness of our own desires.

[333]   5. We can become discerning persons by examining carefully our own experiences. If in reflecting on the course of our thoughts or our actions we find that from beginning to end our eyes have remained fixed on the Lord, we can be sure that the good spirit has been moving us. But if what started off well in our thought and action begins to be self-focused or to turn us from our way to God, we should suspect that the evil spirit has somehow twisted the good beginning to an evil direction and possibly even to an evil end. So we can discover that an original good course has led us to be weakened spiritually or even to become desolate or confused. The signs of desolation give clear indication of the evil spirit's influence.

[334]   6. When we recognize that we have been duped by the evil spirit through a certain thought progression or course of action, we should review carefully all the stages which we passed through from the time

when the evil became apparent back to its very beginnings in the good. By means of such a review, we will find that we can more quickly catch ourselves when we are being led on by the deceit of the evil spirit and so we are more enabled to guard ourselves in the future.

Finally, there are further insights in regard to consolation in the progress of our spiritual life:

7. As we continue to make progress in the spiritual life, the move- [335] ment of the good spirit is very delicate, gentle, and often delightful. It may be compared to the way a drop of water penetrates a sponge.

When the evil spirit tries to interrupt our progress, the movement is violent, disturbing, and confusing. It may be compared to the way a waterfall hits a stone ledge below.

In persons whose lives are going from bad to worse, the descriptions given above should just be reversed. The reason for this lies in the conflict of opposing forces. In other words, when good or evil spirits find our heart a true haven, they enter quietly just as anyone comes into his own home. By contrast, evil spirits cause great commotion and noise as they try to enter into the heart of the just person intent upon the good.

8. When the consolation experience in our life comes directly [336] from God, there can be no deception in it. Although a delight and a peace will be found in such an experience, a spiritual person should be very careful to distinguish the actual moment of this consolation-in-God-himself from the afterglow which may be exhilarating and joyful for some period of time. Quite often it is in this second period of time that we begin to reason out plans of action or to make resolutions which cannot be attributed so directly to God as the initial experience, which is nonconceptual in nature. Because human reasoning and other influences are now coming into the total picture of this consolation period, a very careful process of discerning the good and the evil spirits should be undertaken according to the previous guidelines before any resolution or plan of action is adopted.

Appendix II

WORKSHEET: THE INNER HEART OF MY FAITH

Instructions

Take a moment to look over the worksheet. Using a copy machine, enlarge the worksheet to standard 8½ x 11" size. After you have examined and enlarged it, refer to these instructions for an explanation of the categories found at the top of the worksheet.

1. *Chronology.* Starting at the left column of the worksheet, number down the column in two- or three-year intervals from the year of your birth to the present year.

2. *Basic Philosophy of Life and Key Relationships.* In a phrase, provide a basic description of how you looked at your life experience. Key relationships can be any relationship that you feel had a significant impact on your life at the time. The persons mentioned need not be living now, and you need not have known them personally (that is, they could be persons who influenced you through your reading or hearing about them, etc.).

3. *Major Experiences of Gratitude and Thanksgiving.* What living memories of persons, objects, institutions, events, etc. recall experiences of special gratitude and thanksgiving? Describe simply these heartfelt experiences.

4. *Major Experiences of Sorrow.* What living memories of persons, objects, institutions, events, etc. recall experiences of real sorrow? Describe simply these heartfelt experiences.

5. *Major Experiences of Anxiety and Fear.* Refer to #3 and #4 above.

6. *Major Experiences of Sinfulness.* This is not a segment for listing inappropriately your previous sins, breaking confidentiality. Rather "sinfulness" here refers to naming a disposition in your heart that can actively alienate you or prevent you from receiving a deep-

ening relationship with your true self in Jesus Christ. Name any experience of such an affective disposition in your heart, any interior attitude that prevented you from relating more fully with God, yourself, or your neighbor (e.g., pridefulness, distrust, fear, anger, sloth, greed, envy, lust, gluttony).

7. *Major Experiences of Joy and Love.* Refer to #3 and #4 above.

8. *Image of Self.* Here you can record how you thought and felt about yourself in the environments in which you lived, played, worked, etc. It may be helpful to describe how you spent your time and/or what you thought you were doing at the time.

9. *Icon of God.* This is an invitation for you to record in a phrase or two what your thoughts or images of God were (positive or negative) at different times in your life. If you had no image of God or cannot remember one, answer appropriately.

10. *Heartfelt Revelations, Healings, Teachings.* Here mention any pertinent learning that dawned for you and that significantly affected your growth in faith. Healings should be understood as any experience that significantly enlarged your heart's capacity to receive and to give love.

•

To fill out the worksheet, in each column, use a word, phrase, or brief sentence which expresses your thoughts. It is not necessary to fill out the columns in great detail. If you are unable to complete certain segments, just leave them blank. Remember you are doing the exercise for yourself and to facilitate a spiritual conversation with a spiritual director.

After you have finished your work with the chart, spend some time thinking about your life as a whole. Try to feel its movement and its flow, its continuities and discontinuities, its desolations and consolations. As you look at the worksheet, let yourself imagine your life as a drama or a play. Where would the division of it naturally fall? If you were to divide it into chapters or episodes, how would these be titled? When you have a sense of how your life might be divided, draw lines through these areas on the chart and jot down the titles on the reverse side of the worksheet.

You may have needed to use multiple copies of this worksheet in order to complete this exercise. Please use as many sheets as seems fitting for you to finish. It is quite common for people to use two or three worksheets.

Once completed, this is what James Fowler calls an "Unfolding Tapestry of Life." With permission, I have adapted his reflection instrument to illuminate interior affections active in human experience. Reflection on this experience helps a person become aware of how God's Spirit is active in his or her life. In the coming days or months you may want to return to this, "The Inner Heart of My Faith," for deepening reflection or to add things that may come up to you later. Some people find that this exercise is a good beginning for keeping a regular spiritual journal or diary. You may find too that if you come back to this exercise after some time has passed, the chapters and titles in your life of faith will be different as you look at them in the light of new experiences.

Worksheet: *The Inner Heart of My Faith*

Chronology	Basic Philosophy of Life and Key Relationships	Major Experiences of Gratitude and Thanksgiving	Major Experiences of Sorrow	Major Experiences of Anxiety and Fear	Major Experiences of Sinfulness	Major Experiences of Joy and Love	Image of Self	Icon of God	Heartfelt Revelations, Healings, Teachings

Appendix III

BACKGROUND AID

Toward a Deeper Understanding of the Consciousness Examen: Excerpts from "Consciousness Examen"

For many youth today life is spontaneity if anything. If spontaneity is crushed or aborted, then life itself is stillborn. In this view examen is living life once removed from the spontaneity of life. It is a reflective, dehydrated approach which dries all the spontaneity out of life. These people today disagree with Socrates' claim that the unexamined life is not worth living. For these people the Spirit is in the spontaneous and so anything that militates against spontaneity is un-Spiritual.

This view overlooks the fact that welling up in the consciousness and experience of each of us are two spontaneities, one good and for God, another evil and not for God.

These two types of spontaneous urges and movements happen to all of us. So often the quick-witted, loose-tongued person who can be so entertaining and the center of attention and who is always characterized as being so spontaneous is not certainly being moved by and giving expression to the good spontaneity. For one eager to love God with his or her whole being, the challenge is not simply to let the spontaneous happen but rather to be able to sift out these various spontaneous urges and give full existential ratification to those spontaneous feelings that are from and for God. We do this by allowing the truly Spirited-spontaneity to happen in our daily lives. But we must learn the feel of this true spirited-spontaneity. Examen has a very central role in this learning.

The examen is a time of prayer. The dangers of an empty self-reflection or an unhealthy self-centered introspection are very real.

This appendix is excerpted from George Aschenbrenner, "The Consciousness Examen," *Review for Religious* 31 (1972): 175–78, 183–84. Used with permission.

On the other hand, a lack of effort at examen and the approach of living according to what comes naturally keeps us quite superficial and insensitive to the subtle and profound ways of the Lord deep in our hearts. The prayerful quality and effectiveness of the examen itself depends upon its relationship to the continuing contemplative prayer of the person. Without this relationship examen slips to the level of self-reflection for self-perfection, if it perdures at all.

In daily contemplative prayer the Father reveals to us at His own pace the order of the mystery of all reality in Christ—as Paul says to the Colossians: "those to whom God has planned to give a vision of the full wonder and splendor or his secret plan for the nations" (Col. 1:27). The contemplator experiences in many subtle, chiefly nonverbal, ways this revelation of the Father in Christ. The presence of the Spirit of the risen Jesus in the heart of the believer makes it possible to sense and "hear" this invitation (challenge!) to order ourselves to this revelation. Contemplation is empty without this "ordering" response.

This kind of reverent, docile (the "obedience of faith" Paul speaks of in Romans 16:26), and nonmoralistic ordering is the work of the daily examen — to sense and recognize those interior invitations to the Lord that guide and deepen this ordering from day to day and not to cooperate with those subtle insinuations opposed to that ordering. Without that contemplative contact with the Father's revelation of reality in Christ, both in formal prayer and informal prayerfulness, the daily practice of examen becomes empty; it shrivels up and dies. Without this "listening" to the Father's revelation of His ways which, are so different from our own (Isa. 55:8–9), examen again becomes that shaping up of ourselves which is human and natural self-perfection or, even worse, it can become that selfish ordering of ourselves to our own ways.

Examen without regular contemplation is futile. A failure at regular contemplation emaciates the beautifully rich experience of responsible ordering which the contemplative is continually invited to by the Lord. It is true, on the other hand, that contemplation without regular examen becomes compartmentalized and superficial and stunted in a person's daily living; it is an important means of finding God in everything and not just in the time of formal prayer.

The examen will fundamentally be misunderstood if the goal of this exercise is not grasped. The specific exercise of examen is ultimately aimed at developing a heart with a discerning vision to be active not only for one or two quarter-hour periods in a day but continually. This is a gift from the Lord — a most important one as Solomon realized (1 Kings 3:9–12). So we must constantly pray for this gift, but we must also be receptive to its development within our hearts. A daily practice of examen is essential to this development.

The mature Ignatius near the end of his life was always examining every movement and inclination of his heart, which means he was *discerning* the congruence of everything with his true Christ-centered self. This was the overflow of those regular intensive prayer-exercises of examen every day. The novice or "old-timer" must be aware both of the point of the one or two quarter-hour exercises of examen each day, namely, a continually discerning heart, and of the necessary gradual adaptation of his practice of examen to his stage of development and the situation in the world in which he finds himself. And yet we are all aware of the subtle rationalization of giving up formal examen each day because we have "arrived at" that continually discerning heart. This kind of rationalization will prevent further growth in faith sensitivity to the Spirit and His ways in our daily lives.

When examen is understood and practiced each day, it becomes so much more than just a brief exercise performed once or twice a day. It becomes an exercise which so focuses and renews our specific faith identity that we should be even more reluctant to omit our examen than our formal contemplative prayer each day. Ignatius never talks of omitting it though he does talk of adapting and abbreviating the daily meditation for various reasons. For him it seems the examen was central and quite inviolate. This strikes us as strange until we revamp our understanding of the examen. Then perhaps we begin to see the examen as so intimately connected to our growing identity and so important to finding God in all things at all times that it becomes our central daily experience of prayer.

For Ignatius finding God in all things is what life is all about. Near the end of his life he said that "whenever he wished, at whatever hour, he could find God" (*Autobiography,* #99). This is the mature Ignatius who had so fully allowed God to possess every ounce of his being through a clear YES to the Father that radiated from the very core of his being that he could be conscious at any moment he wanted of the deep peace, joy, and contentment (consolation, see the *Exercises,* #316) which was the experience of God at the center of his heart. Ignatius's identity, at this point in his life, was quite fully and clearly "in Christ" as Paul says: "For now my place is in him, and I am not dependent upon any of the self-achieved righteousness of the Law" (Phil. 3:9); Ignatius knew and was his true self in Christ.

Being able to find God whenever he wanted, Ignatius was able to find Him in all things through a test for congruence of any interior impulse, mood, or feeling with his true self. Whenever he found interior consonance within himself (which registers as peace, joy, contentment again) from the immediate interior movement and felt himself being his true congruent self, then he knew he had heard God's word to him at that instant. And he responded with that fullness of humble courage so typical of Ignatius. If he discovered interior dissonance, agitation, and disturbance "at the bottom of the heart" (to be carefully distinguished from repugnance "at the top of the head") and could not find his true congruent self in Christ, then he recognized the interior impulse as an "evil spirit" and he experienced God by "going against" the desolate impulse (cf. *Exercises*, #319). In this way he was able to find God in all things by carefully discerning all his interior experiences ("spirits"). Thus discernment of spirits became a daily very practical living of the art of loving God with his whole heart, whole body, and whole strength. Every moment of life was loving (finding) God in the existential situation in a deep quiet, peace, and joy.

NOTES

Introduction

1. Harvey Egan, *The Ignatian Mystical Horizon* (St. Louis: Institute of Jesuit Resources, 1976), 129.

2. John O'Donnell, *Hans Urs von Balthasar* (Collegeville, Minn.: Liturgical Press, 1992), 28.

3. Peter J. Kreeft, *Heaven: The Heart's Deepest Longing* (San Francisco: Harper & Row, 1980), 67–68.

4. O'Donnell, *Hans Urs von Balthasar,* 28.

5. Cited in Evelyn Underhill, *Mysticism* (New York: Image Books, Doubleday, 1990), 18–19.

6. Jean Corbon, *The Wellspring of Worship* (New York: Paulist Press, 1988), 146.

Chapter Five: Learnings and Implications

1. Don Saliers, *The Soul in Paraphrase* (Cleveland: OSL Publications, 1991), 21.

2. Ibid., 20.

3. John H. Westerhoff, *Will Our Children Have Faith?* (San Francisco: HarperCollins, 1976), 75.

4. E. F. Schumacher, *A Guide for the Perplexed* (New York: Harper & Row, 1977), 133.

5. Ibid., 129.

6. Ibid., 130–31.

7. Evelyn Underhill, *Practical Mysticism for Normal People* (London: J. P. M. Dent, 1914), 4–5.

8. Saliers, *The Soul in Paraphrase,* 8.

9. Alice Miller, *The Drama of the Gifted Child* (New York: Basic Books, 1981): "What makes us sick are those things we cannot see through, society's constraints that we have absorbed through our mothers eyes" (100).

10. Robert Kegan, *The Evolving Self* (Cambridge, Mass.: Harvard University Presss, 1982): "A profound acknowledgement of our biological reality addresses how we are animated, but it is much more than a theory of motivation. At bottom it is a conception of the life force itself and how we figure in it. Whether from psychoanalysis, genetic biology, or the more recent 'sociobiology,' the prevailing image of our biological reality is, and has been, essentially deterministic

and body based. The theatre of activity is located within each separate, biologically autonomous system (the individual), which carries within itself an inherited code that unfolds (and causes the individual to develop) along a largely predetermined path or sequence. This locating of the individual or separate body as the fundamental source of life's movement contrasts with the behaviorists' notion that tends to place the source of the 'action' in the environment to which the person responds" (43). "I have proposed that we are 'held' throughout our lives in qualitatively different ways as we evolve. The circumstance of being held, I have suggested, reflects not the vulnerable state of infancy but the evolutionary state of embeddedness. However much we evolve, we are always still embedded. Development at any period in the life history, involving an emergence from a psychobiological evolutionary state, must also involve an emergence from embeddedness in a particular human context. This is analogous to transcending my culture and creating a distinction between what now appears as the culture's definition of me and what is 'really me' " (256–57).)

11. M. Scott Peck, *Further Along the Road Less Traveled* (New York: Simon and Schuster, 1993), 246.

12. George E. Vaillant, *The Wisdom of the Ego* (Cambridge, Mass.: Harvard University Press, 1993), 337–38.

13. Jon Sobrino, *Spirituality and Liberation* (Maryknoll, N.Y.: Orbis Books, 1988), 19.

14. Saliers, *The Soul in Paraphrase*, 6.

15. William Lynch, *Christ and Apollo* (Notre Dame, Ind.: University of Notre Dame Press, 1960), 133.

16. Stephen Fields, "Seeing God in the Flesh: Von Balthasar's Recovery of the 'Spiritual Imagination' through His Solution of Two Aporiae of Private Christian Spiritual Experience," paper for scholarly research in the Department of Theology, Yale University, Fall 1991, 12.

17. Saliers, *The Soul in Paraphrase*, 55.

18. John O'Donnell, *Hans Urs von Balthasar* (Collegeville, Minn.: Liturgical Press, 1992), 25.

19. Ibid., 30–31.

Chapter Six: Ministry as Healing, Practical Mysticism

1. Patricia Aburdene and John Naisbitt, *Megatrends 2000* (New York: William Morrow, 1990), 277.

2. Jon Sobrino, *Spirituality and Liberation* (Maryknoll, N.Y.: Orbis Books, 1988), 2.

3. Ibid.

4. James W. Fowler, *Faith Development and Pastoral Care* (Philadelphia: Fortress Press, 1987), 17.

5. Jürgen Moltmann, *The Church in the Power of the Spirit* (San Francisco: Harper & Row, 1991), 214.

6. Ibid., 96.

7. Sobrino, *Spirituality of Liberation*, 126.

8. David L. Fleming, *The Spiritual Exercises of Saint Ignatius Loyola* (St. Louis: Institute of Jesuit Sources, 1989), 22–23.
9. Ibid., 140.
10. Kenneth Leech, *True Prayer* (San Francisco: Harper & Row, 1980), 72.
11. Ibid., 73.
12. Moltmann, *The Church in the Power of the Spirit*, 111.
13. Roberto S. Goizueta, "Liberating Creation Spirituality," *Listening* 24, no. 2 (Spring 1989): 93.
14. Ibid., 94.
15. Pedro Arrupe, *Challenge to Religious Life Today* (St. Louis: Institute for Jesuit Sources, 1979), 206.
16. Karl Rahner, *Sacramentum Mundi: An Encyclopedia of Theology* (New York: Herder and Herder, 1969), s.v. "Mysticism," 137.
17. Ibid.
18. Ibid.
19. Charles Shelton, *Morality of the Heart* (New York: Crossroad, 1990), 62.
20. Ibid.
21. Ibid.
22. *New Catholic Encyclopedia* (New York: McGraw-Hill Book Company, 1967), 11:58. "Pelagianism is a 5th century heresy and is named after Pelagius, its principal author. Divine grace for him is something *external*, as the free will itself, or the precepts of the Old and New Testaments. Its purpose is merely to facilitate *what the will can do by itself*, and it is always given in proportion to one's merits. Pelagianism made God only a spectator (not Indwelling Spirit) in the drama of human salvation."
23. Moltmann, *The Church in the Power of the Spirit*, 90.
24. Pedro Arrupe, *Extemporaneous Remarks at the Bicentennial Gathering of Maryland Province Jesuits* (Philadelphia, 1976).

Chapter Seven: Everyday Prayer and Discernment

1. Jon Sobrino, *Spirituality of Liberation* (Maryknoll, N.Y.: Orbis Books, 1985), 14. Sobrino distinguishes between "theological," and "theologal." "Theological" refers to the study of theology; "theologal" means "related to God."
2. Ibid., 71.
3. George Aschenbrenner, "Consciousness Examen," *Review for Religious* 31 (1972): 14.
4. Ibid., 17.
5. Ibid., 18.
6. Ibid., 20.
7. Ibid.
8. Sobrino, *Spirituality of Liberation*, 40.
9. Ibid., 125.
10. Karl Rahner, *Sacramentum Mundi: An Encyclopedia of Theology* (New York: Herder and Herder, 1969), s.v. "Mysticism," 139.

11. Sobrino, *Spirituality of Liberation*, 41.
12. Ibid.
13. Ibid.
14. Avery Dulles, *Models of the Church* (New York: Image Books, 1987), 103.
15. Ibid., 110.
16. Moltmann, *The Church in the Power of the Spirit*, 110.
17. Ibid., 111-12.

Chapter Eight: Von Balthasar's Trinitarian Theology and Ignatian Prayer

1. Hans Urs von Balthasar, *Prayer* (San Francisco: Ignatius Press, 1986), 177.
2. John O'Donnell, *Hans Urs von Balthasar* (Collegeville, Minn.: Liturgical Press, 1992), 28.
3. Medrad Kehl and Werner Loser, *The Von Balthasar Reader* (New York: Crossroad, 1982), 177.
4. von Balthasar, *Prayer*, 184.
5. Ibid.
6. Ibid.
7. Ibid.
8. Ibid., 185.
9. Ibid., 186.
10. Michael Waldstein, "Hans Urs von Balthasar's Theological Aesthetic," *Communio* (Spring 1985): 23.
11. von Balthasar, *Prayer*, 186.
12. O'Donnell, *Hans Urs von Balthasar*, 26.
13. Kehl and Loser, *The Von Balthasar Reader*, 180.
14. von Balthasar, *Prayer*, 188-89.
15. Ibid., 189.
16. Ibid., 185.
17. Kehl and Loser, *The Von Balthasar Reader*, 180.
18. Ibid., 181.
19. Ibid., 180.
20. von Balthasar, *Prayer*, 197.
21. O'Donnell, *Hans Urs von Balthasar*, 152.
22. von Balthasar, *Prayer*, 193.
23. Hugo Rahner, *Ignatius the Theologian* (New York: Herder and Herder, 1968), 182.
24. Stephen Fields, "Seeing God in the Flesh: Von Balthasar's Recovery of the 'Spiritual Imagination' through His Solution of Two Aporiae of Private Christian Spiritual Experience," paper for scholarly research in the Department of Theology, Yale University, Fall 1991, 11.
25. Ibid., 11.
26. Ibid., 16.

NOTES TO PAGES 137–146

27. Ibid., 17.
28. O'Donnell, *Hans Urs von Balthasar,* 31.
29. Augustine, *Confessions,* Book X, 6 (New York: Penguin Books, 1961), 211.

Chapter Nine: Ignatian Spiritual Direction and Inner Dynamics of the Heart

1. Jean Corbon, *The Wellspring of Worship* (Mahwah, N.J.: Paulist Press, 1988), 73.
2. Maureen Conroy, "On Spiritual Direction," Classroom Handout, Christian Spirituality Program, Creighton University, Omaha, Neb., 1985.
3. Kenneth Leech, *Soul Friend* (San Francisco: Harper & Row, 1980), 34.
4. Martin Thornton, *The Rock and the River* (New York: Morehouse-Barlow, 1965), 141–42.
5. Andrew Tallon, "The Heart in Rahner's Philosophy of Mysticism," *Theological Studies* 53 (1992): 700.
6. Edward Carter, *The Mysticism of Everyday* (Kansas City, Mo.: Sheed and Ward, 1991), 11.
7. "First then, what is this creature we call imagination? To begin with, what is imagination *not?* It is not the same thing as fantasy. Fantasy has come to mean the grotesque, the bizarre. That is fantastic which is unreal, irrational, wild, unrestrained. We speak of 'pure fantasy': It has no connection with reality. It is imagination run wild, on the loose, unbridled, uncontained.

"What is it, then? Imagination is the capacity we have 'to make the material an image of the immaterial or spiritual.' It is a creative power. You find it in Rembrandt's self-portraits, in Beethoven's *Fifth Symphony,* in the odor of a new rose or the flavor of an old wine. You find it in storytellers like C. S. Lewis and Tolkien, in dramatists like Aeschylus and Shakespeare, in poets from Sappho to e. e. cummings.

"Now, when I say 'capacity,' I do not mean a 'faculty' like intellect or will. I mean rather a posture of our whole person toward our experience. It is a way of seeing. It is as with Castaneda, looking for the holes in the world or listening to the space between sounds. It is a breaking through the obvious, the surface, the superficial, to the reality beneath and beyond. It is the world of wonder and intuition, of amazement and delight, of festivity and play" (Walter Burghardt, *Sir, We Would Like to See Jesus* [New York: Paulist Press, 1982], 5).
8. Tallon, "The Heart in Rahner's Philosophy of Mysticism," 711–12.
9. Paul Ricoeur, *Fallible Man* (Chicago: Regnery Gateway, 1965), 200.
10. Ann Ulanov and Barry Ulanov, *Primary Speech* (Atlanta: John Knox Press, 1982), 9.
11. Ibid., 10.
12. Ibid., 11.
13. Ibid., 12.
14. Harvey Egan, *The Ignatian Mystical Horizon* (St. Louis: Institute of Jesuit Sources, 1975), 75–77.

15. George Aschenbrenner, "The Consciousness Examen," *Review for Religious* 31 (1972): 18.

16. James Fowler, *Faith Development and Pastoral Care* (Philadelphia: Fortress Press, 1987), 115.

17. Robert Kegan, *The Evolving Self* (Cambridge, Mass.: Harvard University Press, 1982), 294–96.

18. Alice Miller, *The Drama of the Gifted Child* (New York: Basic Books, 1981), 99–100.

19. Ernest Becker, *The Denial of Death* (New York: Macmillan, 1973), 283–84.

20. Ibid., 285.

21. Ulanov and Ulanov, *Primary Speech*, 29.

22. Ibid., 33.

23. Gerald May, *Addiction and Grace* (San Francisco: HarperCollins, 1988), 179–80.

BIBLIOGRAPHY

Aburdene, Patricia, and John Naisbitt. *Megatrends 2000.* New York: William Morrow, 1990.

Arrupe, Pedro. *Challenge to Religious Life Today.* St. Louis: Institute of Jesuit Sources, 1979.

Aschenbrenner, George A. "Consciousness Examen." *Review for Religious* 31 (1972).

Augustine. *Confessions.* New York: Penguin Books Ltd., 1961.

Barry, William A. *God and You.* New York: Paulist Press, 1987.

———. *Seek My Face.* New York: Paulist Press, 1989.

———, and William J. Connolly. *The Practice of Spiritual Direction.* Minneapolis: Seabury Press, 1982.

Becker, Ernest. *The Denial of Death.* New York: Macmillan, 1973.

Belenky, Mary Field, Blythe McVicker Clinchy, Nancy Rule Goldberger, and Jill Mattuck Tarule. *Women's Ways of Knowing.* New York: Basic Books, 1986.

Browning, Robert L., and Roy A. Reed. *The Sacraments, Religious Education and Liturgy.* Birmingham: Religious Education Press, 1985.

Burghardt, Walter J., S.J. *Sir, We Would Like to See Jesus.* New York: Paulist Press, 1982.

Burns, J. Patout, and Gerald M. Fagin. *The Holy Spirit Message of the Fathers of the Church.* Wilmington, Del.: Michael Glazier, 1984.

Burrows, Ruth. *Guidelines for Mystical Prayer.* Denville, N.J.: Dimension Books, 1976. See chapter 4: "A Look at Experiences," chapter 5: "The Hold-Up," and chapter 6: "The Roots and Branches of Sin."

Carter, Edward. *The Mysticism of Everyday.* Kansas City, Mo.: Sheed and Ward, 1991.

Clark, Mary T. *Augustine of Hippo: Selected Writings from the "Confessions" and "On the Trinity."* Classics of Western Spirituality. New York: Paulist Press, 1984.

Congar, Yves. *I Believe in the Holy Spirit: Lord and Giver of Life.* Vol. 2. New York: Seabury Press, 1983.

Conroy, Maureen. *Growing in Love and Freedom.* Denville, N.J.: Dimension Books, 1987.

———"The Role of Consolation and Desolation." Classroom handout, Summer 1984, Christian Spirituality Program, Creighton University, Omaha, Neb.

———. "On Spiritual Direction." Classroom handout, Summer 1985, Christian Spirituality Program, Creighton University, Omaha, Neb.

Corbon, Jean. *The Wellspring of Worship.* New York: Paulist Press, 1988.

Cusson, Giles. *Biblical Theology and the Spiritual Exercises*. St. Louis: Institute of Jesuit Sources, 1988.

Dulles, Avery. *Models of the Church*. New York: Image Books, 1987.

Dupré, Louis, and James A. Wiseman, O.S.B. *Light from Light*. New York: Paulist Press, 1988.

Egan, Harvey D. *The Spiritual Exercises and the Ignatian Mystical Horizon*. St. Louis: Institute of Jesuit Sources, 1976.

Erikson, Erik. *Toys and Reasons*. New York: W. W. Norton, 1977.

Faricy, Robert. *Praying*. Minneapolis: Winston Press, 1979.

Ferder, Fran. *Words Made Flesh*. Notre Dame, Ind.: Ave Maria Press, 1986.

Fields, Stephen. "Seeing God in the Flesh: Von Balthasar's Recovery of the 'Spiritual Imagination' through His Solution of Two Aporiae of Private Christian Spiritual Experience." Paper for scholarly research in the Department of Theology, Yale University, New Haven, Conn., Fall 1991.

Fleming, David L. *The Spiritual Exercises of Saint Ignatius Loyola*. St. Louis: Institute of Jesuit Sources, 1989.

Fowler, James W. *Faith Development and Pastoral Care*. Philadelphia: Fortress Press, 1987.

————. *Stages of Faith*. San Francisco: HarperSanFrancisco, 1981.

————. *Weaving the New Creation*. San Francisco: HarperCollins, 1991.

Geertz, Clifford. *The Interpretation of Cultures*. San Francisco: HarperCollins, 1973. See chapter 4: "Religion as a Cultural Symbol," and chapter 5: "Ethos, World View, and the Analysis of Sacred Symbols."

Goizueta, Roberto S. "Liberating Creation Spirituality." *Listening: Journal of Religion and Culture* 24, no. 2 (1989).

Green, Thomas H. *Weeds among Wheat*. Notre Dame, Ind.: Ave Maria Press, 1964.

Griffin, Emile. *Turning*. New York: Image Books, 1982.

Groeschel, Benedict J. *Spiritual Passages*. New York: Crossroad, 1984.

Groome, Thomas. *Sharing Faith*. San Francisco: HarperCollins, 1991.

Harrington, Daniel J. *God's People in Christ*. Philadelphia: Fortress Press, 1980.

Harris, Maria. *Fashion Me a People*. Louisville: John Knox Press, 1989.

Hauser, Richard J. *Moving in the Spirit*. New York: Paulist Press, 1986.

James, William. *The Varieties of Religious Experience*. New York: Random House, 1929.

Jampolsky, Gerald G. *Love Is Letting Go of Fear*. Berkeley, Calif.: Celestial Arts, 1979.

Kegan, Robert. *The Evolving Self*. Cambridge, Mass.: Harvard University Press, 1982.

Kehl, Medrad, and Werner Loser. *The Von Balthasar Reader*. New York: Crossroad, 1982.

Kelsey, Morton. *The Other Side of Silence*. New York: Paulist Press, 1976. See chapter 14: "Developing Imagination: Stepping into the Inner World," chapter 15: "A Check List for the Venture Inward," and chapter 16: "Putting the Imagination to Work."

Kreeft, Peter J. *Heaven: The Heart's Deepest Longing*. San Francisco: Harper & Row, 1980.

Leech, Kenneth. *Soul Friend*. San Francisco: Harper & Row, 1977.

———. *True Prayer*. San Francisco: Harper & Row, 1989.

Lewis, C. S. *The Weight of Glory*. New York: Macmillan, 1965.

Link, Mark. *Journey*. Allen, Tex.: Tabor Publishing, 1970.

Lynch, William F. *Christ and Apollo*. Notre Dame, Ind.: University of Notre Dame Press, 1960.

———. *Images of Hope*. Notre Dame, Ind.: University of Notre Dame Press, 1965.

Maas, Robin, and Gabriel O'Donnell. *Spiritual Traditions for the Contemporary Church*. Nashville: Abingdon Press, 1990.

May, Gerald G. *Addiction and Grace*. San Francisco: HarperCollins, 1988.

———. *Care of Mind Care of Spirit*. San Francisco: Harper & Row, 1982.

Meeks, Douglas M. *God the Economist*. Minneapolis: Fortress Press, 1989.

Metz, Johann Baptist. *The Emergent Church*. New York: Crossroad, 1985.

Miller, Alice. *The Drama of the Gifted Child*. New York: Basic Books, 1981.

Moltmann, Jürgen. *The Church in the Power of the Spirit*. San Francisco: Harper & Row, 1991.

———. *The Trinity and the Kingdom*. San Francisco: Harper & Row, 1981.

Moore, Sebastian. *Jesus the Liberator of Desire*. New York: Crossroad, 1989.

O'Donnell, John. *Hans Urs von Balthasar*. Collegeville, Minn.: Liturgical Press, 1992.

Otto, Rudolf. *The Idea of the Holy*. New York: Oxford University Press, 1958.

Peck, M. Scott. *Further Along the Road Less Traveled*. New York: Simon and Schuster, 1993.

Percy, Walker. *The Message in the Bottle*. New York: Farrar, Straus and Giroux, 1987. See chapter 8: "Toward a Triadic Theory of Meaning," and chapter 9: "The Symbolic Structure of Interpersonal Process."

Potter-Efron, Ronald, and Patricia Potter-Efron. *Letting Go of Shame*. New York: Harper & Row, 1989.

Powell, John. *The Secret of Staying in Love*. Allen, Tex.: Tabor Publishing, 1974.

Pruyser, Paul W. *The Minister as Diagnostician*. Philadelphia: Westminster Press, 1976.

Rahner, Hugo. *Ignatius the Theologian*. New York: Herder and Herder, 1968.

Rahner, Karl. *Faith in Practice*. New York: Crossroad, 1989.

———. *Faith Today*. London: Sheed and Ward, 1967.

———. *Foundations of Christian Faith*. New York: Crossroad, 1978. See chapter 2: "Man in the Presence of Absolute Mystery," chapter 3: "Man as a Being Threatened Radically by Guilt," chapter 4: "Man as the Event of God's Free and Forgiving Self-Communication," and chapter 8: "Remarks on the Christian Life."

———. *A Rahner Reader*. Ed. Gerald A. McCool. New York: Crossroad, 1984.

———. *Sacramentum Mundi: An Encyclopedia of Theology*. New York: Herder and Herder, 1969. S.v. "Mysticism."

———. *Theological Investigations*. Volume 3: *Theology of the Spiritual Life*. Baltimore: Helicon Press, 1967.

Ricoeur, Paul. *Fallible Man*. Chicago: Regnery Gateway, 1965.

Rohr, Richard, and Andreas Ebert. *Discovering the Enneagram*. New York: Crossroad, 1991.

St. Romain, Philip. *Becoming a New Person — Twelve Steps to Christian Growth*. Liguori, Mo.: Liguori Publications, 1984.

Saliers, Don E. *The Soul in Paraphrase*. Cleveland: OSL Publications, 1991.

Sampson, William, S.J. *The Coming of Consolation*. Westminster, Md.: Christian Classics, 1986.

Schumacher, E. F. *A Guide for the Perplexed*. New York: Harper & Row, 1977.

Shelton, Charles M. *Morality of the Heart*. New York: Crossroad, 1990.

Sobrino, Jon. *Spirituality of Liberation*. Maryknoll, N.Y.: Orbis Books, 1985.

Tallon, Andrew. "The Heart in Rahner's Philosophy of Mysticism." *Theological Studies* 53 (1992).

Thornton, Martin. *Christian Proficiency*. Cambridge, Mass.: Cowley Publications, 1988.

———. *The Rock and the River*. New York: Morehouse-Barlow Company, 1965.

Ulanov, Ann, and Barry Ulanov. *Primary Speech*. Atlanta: John Knox Press, 1982.

Underhill, Evelyn. *Mysticism*. New York: Image Books, Doubleday, 1990.

———. *Practical Mysticism for Normal People*. London: J. P. M. Dent, 1914.

Vaillant, George E. *The Wisdom of the Ego*. Cambridge, Mass.: Harvard University Press, 1993.

Vanier, Jean. *Community and Growth*. New York: Paulist Press, 1979.

Viviano, Benedict T., O.P. *The Kingdom of God in History*. Wilmington, Del.: Michael Glazier, 1988.

Von Balthasar, Hans Urs. *Heart of the World*. San Francisco: Ignatius Press, 1979.

———. *Prayer*. San Francisco: Ignatius Press, 1986.

Waldstein, Michael. "Hans Urs von Balthasar's Theological Aesthetic," *Communio* (Spring 1985).

Westerhoff, John H. *Will Our Children Have Faith?* San Francisco: Harper-Collins, 1976.

Yarnold, Edward. *The Awe Inspiring Rites of Initiation: Selected writings from the Baptismal Homilies of Cyril of Jerusalem, Ambrose, John Chrysostom, and Theodore of Mopsuestia*. Slough, U.K.: St. Paul Publications, 1971.